Nexus:

A Book About
Youth Work

CURRENT PRINTING (last digit)
10 9 8 7 6 5 4 3 2 1

Cover Art by Suzanne Vande Boom
Applauding Rain Studio

Text Design and Page Layout
by Sean M. Young

A Publication of the Child and Youth Care Learning Center
Division of Outreach and Continuing Education

University of Wisconsin–Milwaukee
P.O Box 413
Milwaukee, WI 53201

in partnership with

Child Welfare League of America, Inc.
440 First Street, N.W.
Suite 310
Washington, DC 20001–2085

ISBN 0-9646955-0-2

Acknowledgements

Thanks to all the workers for their stories. Thanks also to
Suzanne, as always, for the art work and inspiration;
to Henry Maier, who read, reread and made helpful suggestions
as the book progressed; to Mike Baizerman, who after hearing
me describe the themes for the untitled manuscript, called them
a value nexus; to Gerry Fewster for his courage and tenacity
about being in child and youth care; and to Mary Drees for
helping make it ring true.

Table of Contents

Introduction

Youth work with at–risk youths is largely existential, experiential, and developmental. It takes place in the here and now as workers use their experience and knowledge of human development to weave as much care, learning, and counseling as possible into their daily interactions.

Each interaction and/or moment has tremendous potential. A worker putting his hand on a youth's shoulder and leading the way out the door. A worker sitting quietly on a couch reading with a youth. A group of youths running together. A smile. A conversation. A crisis.

When it goes well, youth workers and youths are in sync with each other's rhythms for trusting and growing. They are present and acting with purpose.

At other times, youth work is a struggle. A gut-wrenching, frightening struggle that takes courage and desire to resolve.

In this book, youth work theories, techniques, and themes are described within the context of a twenty-four hour period at an agency with several community and group care programs for at-risk teenagers. My hope is that it will provide a forum for learning and reaffirming many of the central actions and attitudes in effective youth work practice.

Nexus:
  1. connection, link
  2. a connected group or series

Definition of Nexus for this book:
  1. a series of interwoven actions, feelings, and attitudes
  2. the name of the agency in chapters two and three with several programs for at-risk teenagers

Chapter One:
Framing Youth Work as a Story

"Consider that youthwork is a story, a narrative structure that gives form and substance to youthwork practice....."

-Baizerman (1992, p. 30).

1

Youth workers often tell stories. Stories put their work in context, providing the necessary flow and atmosphere. The readers or listeners or tellers can get a feel and understanding for what the work is like.

Story is also a metaphor for youth work. Each day the story builds through a series of interactions that include four central elements:

Rhythm

Rhythm is beat, motion, tempo. Workers and youths moving through the day in and out of sync—a series of upbeats and downbeats. The movement of a group of teenagers from one activity to the next at an easy pace. A discussion of what is to come (foreshadowing) conducted in a firm, reassuring voice. The movement of hands mirroring the flow of the moment.

A steady tone of voice that calms rather than excites; or a staccato, jubilant voice encouraging youths to participate in an activity.

A body positioned and moving to quell an attack or provide a safe zone of expression. A nonthreatening hand reaching out to assist. A "quick step" and a grasp to avoid being hit.

Entering a youth's room in the morning or the beginning of a shift at a pace that is sensitive to the youth's emotional preparedness to be greeted and to greet. Leaving at night or the end of the shift at a pace that conveys a sense of continuation.

A football tossed back and forth at a steady pace with smooth follow–throughs. A change in tempo to maintain the enthusiasm. A hand moving to greet the hand of one youth, then another who is reaching for the bowl of french fries. A walk in the woods conducted at a pace that everyone can keep up with, not so fast to exclude or so slow as to lose enthusiasm.

A jog starting out slowly enough not to exhaust the runners before the easy, almost effortless, second wind arrives, then becoming a run in which legs and arms move in harmony with one another and the surface of the street or field. A conversation with pauses and starts that invites the entry of another voice. Eyes moving from one youth to another during a group discussion. A head nodding with words of encouragement and assurance. A body shifting to evoke further participation. Other heads and bodies joining in.

The comforting rhythm of a song at bedtime, the invigorating rhythm of another song during an activity. The rhythm in a dance that helps sooth a broken heart or unleash pent-up anger. Guitars strummed and feet moving together to a variety of songs and dances to connect children with the group and their family and culture.

Presence

Workers often speak of the need to be "real." Presence is being real or bringing a desire to know and continually discover oneself to the mutual boundaries where relationships are formed. It seems to come as much from the quest to understand oneself as it does from the amount of awareness and skill one has in expressing self. A person who is searching to know himself or herself is more real than one who is not. The search is part of who one is, however, not necessarily a constant process of conscious self-examination. People who are consumed by self are not present.

Presence is also being there with conviction and the knowledge that children who have been physically and psychologically abandoned throughout their lives need committed, dependable, predictable adults whom they can count on.

"You either throw yourself into it body and soul or you forget it. There can be no compromise."
(Waggoner, 1984, p. 255)

Fewster (1991) teaches that youth work is a shared journey: worker and youth going through the day searching and trying to discover themselves. In the journey, the worker, who is the more experienced traveler, leads by being present and aware until eventually the youth finds his or her own path.

Presence is also being *with* children and families:

"Youthworkers ... don't build trust mechanically, like carpenters build houses: they are in the world with youth and, in so being, disclose trust as fundamental to being together as persons ..."

(Baizerman, 1992, p. 132).

Presence is conveyed by eyes, smiles and nods that are alert and attentive. By an honest expression of how one feels. By listening intently, with eye contact and feedback. By showing up for work on time. By enthusiasm during activities and routines. By being predictable and dependable.

It is also conveyed by expressions of self–confidence and the will to hang in there during a crisis. By firmness. By the conscious and unconscious quest to know oneself. By a quiver of the voice that alerts a worker to an unresolved issue or underlying fear. By awareness of how one's feelings about abandonment, attachment, success and failure influence one's interactions and the ability to adjust one's actions accordingly to meet the needs of youth who have been severely abused and have experienced considerable abandonment and rejection. By using this awareness of self to be more aware of and sensitive to others' feelings. By the underlying message: we can move forward together, you and I. I am confident based on my experience and knowledge of your needs that we can make it. You are safe, because I am here and will go with you. I will try to know myself if you will try to know yourself.

Meaning

Bruner (1990) argues that in order to understand humans, we have to understand how experiences and acts are shaped by intentional states and that the form of these intentional states is realized through participation in the symbolic systems of culture.

> *"Indeed, the very shape of our lives—the rough and changing draft of our autobiography that we carry in our minds—is understandable to ourselves and others only by those cultural systems of interpretation"*
>
> (Bruner, 1990, p. 33).

In the moments and interactions being discussed here, meaning can be defined as acting with purpose in the context of one's cultural or familial or social experience. A way of moving, a gesture, a spoken word, a ritual or a way of solving a problem that has meaning within one's past or present family, group, community life. It is also the meaning arrived at through what has been referred to as a mutually constructed reality or the common ground that is sometimes needed for two or more people to communicate and solve problems. Meaning is also the sense of two people who are acting together with a positive purpose, even if the purpose or meaning of the action is different for each participant.

A worker or youth acts because he or she believes it is right to act and that the actions will bring fulfillment for oneself as well as others. A worker and youth find a common purpose and act together because they believe it is best. A worker or youth acts because the actions create something that feels familiar or good or safe. A piece of bread buttered, a collar buttoned or unbuttoned, a phrase delivered, a ball batted, or a fork held in a certain way because it evokes these feelings. Or perhaps a problem is resolved or an effort undertaken in a way that one believes will lead to the best results.

A sense of meaning or purpose is conveyed by workers to youths and often vice versa through actions and words. Through reframing a situation so that there is common, or acceptance of different, purpose. Through contentment or joy or enthusiasm. Through conviction. Through confidence that what one is doing is wholesome and good. Through actions that are consistent with the intended purpose. Through the message: We are doing this together, with meaning, you and I. The process and the outcome of our actions will be fruitful. I understand that it might have a different meaning for you, but I hope and believe it will be fulfilling.

Atmosphere

Atmosphere is space, time, surroundings. It is also tone and mood. Maier (1987) writes that the space we create defines us and helps bring people together, to be in touch with and aware of each other, and to engage in parallel activities. He also writes that space provides distance when needed.

Atmosphere, of course, can enhance most interactions. A light turned down to quiet the group. A radio turned up to invigorate. Rooms decorated with children's paintings and posters to encourage expression and to help provide a sense of safety and familiarity. Reds, blues, and yellows to liven things up. Earth tones to ground. Chairs placed in a circle to facilitate discussion and participation. A room or hallway sized properly for an activity. A window left open or closed for comfort.

Workers also create atmosphere with the tones of their voices. The expressions on their faces. A mood that sends off good vibes. Or a sense of being and confidence that evokes permanence and safety. We are in this space, you and I, and together we create, change, and shape it for our mutual benefit.

In the story of youth work, interactions take place in five key periods:

Transitions

Youth work has many transitions. Workers and youths move from one activity to another. A day or shift or activity begins and ends. The tempo of an activity or a facial expression changes. Workers move with youths from the play yard to the dinner table, from showers to bed, from night to day, from checkers to basketball, from the classroom to the recreation area, from the community center or group home to home, and so forth.

These movements, changes, beginnings, and endings often evoke memories and feelings related to separation, loss, abandonment, failure, unfulfilled dreams, and interrupted opportunities. Disturbed and at–risk children have often been psychologically and physically abandoned. Their lives have been a series of unsuccessful transitions. They have been kicked out, left behind, and pushed away. They have also had their hopes dashed time and again. Thus, they are often anxious, afraid, angry, sad, and skeptical of change.

When they enter a group home or community program, it is hard for them to trust people because they don't believe people will stay and treat them differently. It often takes many months before they can allow themselves to attach to others without the fear of being abandoned or hurt again.

A portion of their fear of abandonment and attachment is overcome by experiencing a series of successful changes, comings and goings, beginnings and endings, enterings and leavings in which they learn to be able to count on and trust adults.

Activities

Youth workers are engaged with children in a variety of recreation, counseling, decision–making and daily living activities. In each of these activities, from the smallest to the largest and the shortest to the longest, there is a chance to care, counsel, teach, and empower. Thus, workers try to gear activities to the social, emotional, cognitive, and physical developmental needs of each youth and the conditions or circumstances surrounding their interactions. Gymnastics is chosen because it is better suited to the group members' skills and attitudes at a certain moment than baseball. An art project is chosen as an opportunity for expression instead of a rap session because the time, mood, and mode of expression are better. Routines—mealtimes, bedtimes, and chores—are planned and conducted to build trusting relationships and skills according to each youth's needs. Music, dance, art and recreation activities are planned with sensitivity to cultural and familial backgrounds. And so forth.

Counseling

Workers counsel youth throughout the day. A worker who has just encouraged a youth not to run away talks to the youth about his fears at bedtime and explores ways in which the youth can express his fear without running away or hurting someone. A youth shares his feelings about being abandoned in a group meeting. A fight is prevented by workers helping two youths express their anger without going to blows. During dinner a youth is encouraged to express how he feels without blaming others.

Crises

Crises occur frequently in youth work. At-risk youth lash out, run away, steal, or trash. An activity is interrupted by a fight. A youth returns from home angry and takes it out on his roommate. A drug dealer comes after one of his runners. A youth is shot for his jacket. A parent beats a youth.

Workers try to create a safe environment. They do everything they can to prevent problems, but sometimes they have to intervene with physical and emotional support.

Although often frightened and angry themselves, the workers try not to react the way others have reacted. They do not take a youth's behavior personally and they try to convey the message that they understand how a youth feels even though they do not accept the behavior. They try to teach youths how to express their feelings in a safer, more productive way.

Teamwork

As workers work with other workers and members of other disciplines, their interactions with one another are interwoven with their interactions with communities and families. In other words, when team members are praising, encouraging, and supporting one another, this has a positive influence on how they praise, encourage, and support the youths and families they are trying to help. When team members can help a member who is struggling, they are more likely to be able to help families and communities acknowledge their roles in helping a youth who is struggling.

Likewise, when a team is dysfunctional it mirrors dysfunctional communities and families. When team members blame, push someone out, or victimize, they are not very likely to be able to help families and communities that do the same. The challenge is to be aware of these cycles of positive and negative interaction and to interact with one another in a way workers would like parents, neighbors, and youths to interact with one another.

A Metaphor: Basketball

Three youths and Matt, a youth worker, walk to the playground for a game of two-on-two basketball. It is a familiar walk, one that they make three or four times a week together.

Nick, one of the youths, is worried about leaving. In a few weeks he'll be going to a foster home. But, as they walk towards the playground tossing and bouncing the ball his thoughts are on the game.

It is a warm early fall day. Ron and Pat, the two other youths, decide to play against Matt and Nick. They warm up shooting jumpers and hook shots. One or another crouches in a defensive position in front of the other trying playfully to block a shot.

The early moments of the game go smoothly, as if choreographed by its previous history. The score bounces back and forth. A shot is blocked, a rebound grabbed, a ball falls cleanly through the net. As they jostle for position and dive for loose balls they seem to have an innate sense for each other's positions. Throughout, Matt is in the center of their movements.

After about 45 minutes, with the score tied, they take a break and drink from the jar of ice water Matt prepared before the game. Nick sits next to Matt on the asphalt with his back against the chain link fence. Pat and Ron stand nearby. Sweat has filled their T shirts.

As they rib one another about an errant pass or a missed shot, the visit creeps back into Nick's mind. Sensing this, Matt shifts a bit closer and hands Nick the jar. Suddenly Nick stands and bats the ball from Ron's hands and the game is on again.

In the second half the pace intensifies. The leads widen. First one team is ahead, then the other. In an attempt to regain the lead, Nick shoves Pat as Pat goes for the ball. "Cool it," Matt says, positioning himself between the two and holding the ball a second before putting it back in play.

On the next inbounds, Ron scores on a hook shot, putting his team four up. Matt bounce passes to Nick in the corner. He goes up for a jumper. Pat times his leap perfectly and tips the ball as it leaves Nick's hand.

"Foul!" Nick shouts.

"Bull, it was clean," Pat responds.

"Fuck you!"

"What?" Pat walks slowly towards Nick.

"I said fuck you!" Nick says.

They get in each other's faces. Matt steps between them again and straightens his arms to create some distance. Ron stands by the side with the ball on his hip.

"He's just worried about leaving," Pat says.

"No I'm not, fuck face," Nick responds.

"All right cool it. Let's take a break. Nick, settle yourself down," Matt says, sensing his own anger is about to get the best of him.

"I don't need to settle down. He's the one who fouled me." Nick points at Pat.

"Ron and Pat, take a few," Matt instructs them to take some practice shots at the other end of the court.

"C'mon," Matt motions for Nick to follow him over to the fence near the jar of water.

"What are you talking to me for, he's the one who started it," Nick mumbles as he slowly follows.

Matt takes a drink and hands the jar to Nick. "Look, I understand about leaving. But it won't help to get into it with Pat. If you want to talk, I'm here to listen."

"I don't want to talk about it now."

"Okay, later, but then cool it."

Nick looks down at his shoes, then slowly circles. Matt waits a moment, then looks at him. He nods.

"Okay, lets get rolling," Matt shouts to the others.

Pat and Ron trot down the court with the ball. "Take it out," Matt says and the game regains it's earlier rhythm.

This story has interactions and/or moments with rhythm, presence, meaning, atmopshere. It also has transitions, activity, counseling, a crisis, and teamwork. A youth is worried. He forgets and feels connected as he moves together with a worker and his peers in a familiar activity. At first the flow of the game is smooth, but then the tempo changes. The youth begins to worry again. He lashes out. A worker acknowledges the youth's fear and anger while being aware of his own. He intervenes in a firm but caring way. A conflict is resolved. The journey continues.

In the following chapters, youth work will be described during one twenty-four-hour period.

Chapter Two
Nexus: Afternoon and Evening

The following story takes place from one afternoon to the next at Nexus, a multifaceted agency for at-risk youth. Like youth work, it contains a considerable amount of movement and dialogue. The best way to learn from the story is to pause at points to reflect on and/or discuss what is happening in a scene, then return again later and analyze the interactions in relationship to central elements (rhythm, presence, meaning, and atmosphere) and key periods of interaction (transitions, activities, counseling, crisis, and teamwork) in Chapter One and the additional themes in Chapter Four.

Introductions:

The Nexus Street Corner Program

Hank, a Nexus street worker

Nate, a gang leader

The Nexus Group Home

Matt, Nicole, Jack, Bonny, and Tony (youth workers)

Josh, Pat, Ron, Jennifer, Monique, and Nick (youths)

Mr. and Mrs. Wilson (Josh's parents)

The Nexus Independent Living Program

Milly and Louisa (youth workers)

Tanya, Nathan, Tad, Lamont, and Angel (youths)

The Nexus In–Home Program

Ramon and Natalie (youth workers)

Jessica, Renee, and Paul (siblings)

Mr. and Mrs. McNight (parents)

Since there are several characters in the story, in scenes where several people are involved, youth workers are designated by the letters (yw) and youths by the letter (y) so workers and youths are not confused.

Nexus

A street corner conversation

It's a fall day in the midwest. On the playground, Hank, a Nexus youth worker, is talking to Nate, a local gang leader, a big, restless-looking young man.

"Why don't you help us with this project?" Hank asks.

"Shit man, what you trying to do, get a grant?" Nate leans against the school building.

"What do you mean?" Hank asks.

"Every time somebody comes down here to work with us, they're trying to get a grant. Then after the money runs out, they're gone... Give us the money, man. We'll make sure the neighborhood is safe."

"This isn't a grant," Hank smiles.

"What is it then?"

"An offer to work together."

"What's in it for us?"

"The feeling that you are doing something worthwhile."

"Fuck, man..." Nate begins to walk away, then turns and looks into Hank's eyes, "What's in it for you?"

Hank searches for something to say.

Making decisions

At the Nexus Group Home across the street five youth workers, Matt, Nicole, Jack, Bonny, and Tony, are sitting in a circle on the living room floor, finishing a daily team meeting. A bowl of fruit has been placed on the dining room table. It is a two-story, frame house with bedrooms upstairs and a living room, kitchen, and dining room on the ground floor.

"I agree," Matt says.

"Are you sure it's safe?" Tony asks.

"Yes, I think so," Jack answers. "The supervised visits have gone well."

"You'll be available just in case won't you, Jack?" Bonny, the team leader, asks.

"Yes, of course."

"What about you, Nicole, what do you think?" Bonny looks at Nicole, the newest team member.

"I'm concerned too, but I think it is important for him to spend as much time as possible at home now."

"So, we are all in agreement? Josh will go on a home visit this weekend?" Bonny asks.

They all nod.

The youths, four boys and two girls, arrive shortly and stretch out on the furniture with bananas and apples. Like most troubled youths, they have been victims of abuse and neglect. Their faces, though, show the tired look that comes at the end of a day at school. One of the youths, Franco, is not present. He ran away two days ago.

"So how was the field trip to the museum," Nicole (yw) asks.

"Boring," Ron, a gangly 16-year-old, says.

"I liked it, especially the modern exhibits," Monique, a 15-year-old, follows.

As they chat, Jack, a youth worker, approaches Josh, the boy who will be having the home visit. "Can I speak with you a minute outside?"

Josh (y) looks up from the music cassettes he's been looking through. "Sure, I guess so."

They sit on the porch steps under the cover of an old oak tree. Bonny (the supervisor) and Tony (yw), who worked the morning shift, leave for supervision. They stop to talk with Jack (yw) and Josh (y) a few minutes, then walk down the street to the Nexus headquarters, which is a block away.

"We've decided it's time for you to go on a home visit," Jack (yw) says to Josh (y).

"Great." Josh's eyes lift.

"I'm glad you're pleased."

"How long?"

"Noon Saturday until noon Sunday."

"Cool."

"I'll be on call in case you feel you need to talk or want to return."

"I know." Josh jumps down the stairs and turns towards Jack. "What will we do?"

"I have some football tickets."

"Will my dad go?"

"I'll ask when I go over there later."

Inside, Nicole (yw) has moved to the dining room table with the two girls and one of the boys to begin a story writing activity.

"Think about the image of that time when you felt happy, sad, strong or weak," Nicole says. The youths reflect.

"Now think of what you heard, saw, and smelled."

Again, they reflect.

"Now begin to write without stopping to correct yourself; just write whatever comes to your mind."

As they write, Josh (y), joins Matt (yw), and two other boys, Ron and Pat, for basketball at the playground across the street. Jack (yw) goes to visit Josh's parents.

Helping them make it on their own

The Nexus Headquarters, a former neighborhood grocery store, is equally busy with activity. Bonny and Tony are meeting for weekly supervision in Bonny's office. Louisa, a referral worker, is on the phone trying to connect several children and families with health, social, and job services. Milly, the independent living worker, is preparing for independent living support group, a weekly meeting for seven 18- to 20-year-olds who have moved from Nexus' transitional living home and are trying to make it on their own.

Tanya, a sassy, energetic, 18–year–old arrives early with her daughter on her hip. "That asshole turned off my fucking heat," she says to Milly (yw), referring to the landlord of the flat she shares with two other girls.

"Here, let's talk to Louisa (yw) and see what you can do."

"I know who to call." Louisa (yw) looks through her list of phone numbers and hands Tanya (y) a couple. "Try to clean up your language a little bit," she advises Tanya.

18

The other kids arrive a few minutes apart. While they wait for the meeting to start, they eat snacks and meet with Louisa, who helps them search through the notices and want ads for a job, a lamp, a mattress, some canned goods.

Tad, one of the independent living support group members, introduces his roommate, Lamont, to Milly. But as she is about to greet him, the phone rings.

"Excuse me," she says and picks up the receiver. "Hello, this is Milly Townsend."

"He beat me up again." There are tears in Angel's, one of the independent living group members, voice.

"Hold it a minute, Angel." Milly (yw) covers the receiver with her hand. "Tad, why don't you get Lamont something to eat, I'll be there in a minute." The boys walk to the used refrigerator in the corner. "Are you okay?" Milly (yw) asks Angel (y).

"Yes, I think so, but I need somewhere to live."

"Have you called the police?"

"No, I can't."

"You have to report it."

"Don't you have a room?"

"Yes, there is a room at the independent living flat, but first you have to check in at the woman's shelter."

"But they'll notify the police."

"Yes."

"That will only make it worse."

"Angel, no one can help you if you aren't willing to help your- self. I know how lonely you are, but staying with an abusive man is not the answer. Besides, you'll be safe at the shelter."

"He'll find me there; it doesn't matter where I go."

"Not if the police are notified."

"They won't do anything, I know it... Let me stay at the flat, Milly."

"Angel, I can't put the other kids at risk."

Angel starts crying hysterically.

"I know how frightened you are... I'll help, but you're 19 now. You have to start taking responsibility for your own well being."

Angel continues to cry. "I know, I know."

"Look, come down here. We'll talk and then after support group I'll take you to the woman's shelter."

"I thought you had other appointments," Angel sobs.

"I'll rearrange things."

"Okay," Angel wipes her tears.

"Promise."

"Yes."

"Good." Milly hangs up.

"Who was it?" Nathan (y) asks.

"Angel."

"I thought so; is she coming?"

"Yes. Let's all sit down."

Dressed in worn but colorful vests, hats and tennis shoes, the group members sit around a table with fruit and snacks.

"How has it been going?" Milly (yw) asks.

"I got a job," Bill (y) begins.

"You did? Where?"

"Cleaning carpets."

"How much?" Nathan (y) asks.

"$6.50 an hour."

"Not bad...."

20

They continue to report on how they are doing. As they talk Milly (yw) suggests churches and other organizations where they can get help and resources.

"Did you hear about that girl who got shot for her jacket," Nadine (y) says at one point.

"I knew her, that was Cindy." Tanya (y) shifts her baby, who has begun to cry. "It's always happening," Tanya says.

Tension/resolution

The basketball game with the kids from the group home is tied. Matt, the youth worker, and Ron (y) are playing against Pat (y) and Josh (y). Ron times his jump perfectly and blocks Josh's shot.

"Foul," Josh shouts.

"It was clean!" Ron says.

"Bull!" Josh pushes Ron.

Matt gets in between them. "It was a clean block, Josh."

"Fuck!" Josh says.

Ron stares him down. Josh pushes him. "All right, cool it!" Matt says.

Josh walks to the chain link fence.

"You're just worried about your visit," Ron says.

"No I'm not, fuck face!"

"I said that's enough!" Matt moves towards Josh. "If you are worried, I understand, but fighting isn't the way to show it."

"I said I wasn't worried."

"All right then, settle down."

In a few minutes, Josh returns to the court, "I'm cool. Let's go."

Matt looks at Ron and Josh, then puts the ball back in play.

Writing stories

In the group home, Nicole (yw) leans over Nick's (y) shoulder, examining the metaphor, "like a wild man," he used in the middle of his story. "Why did you choose that one to describe yourself at that moment?" she asks.

Nick thinks a moment. Monique (y) and Jennifer (y) remain engrossed in their own stories.

"Because that's how I felt...." Nick says.

Supervision

In Bonny's office at the headquarters, Tony and Bonny are talking about the group meeting last night. Monique, one of the kids who always asks what's on her mind, asked Tony if he slept with his girlfriend.

"So, how did you respond," Bonny asks.

"I told her it wasn't socially proper to ask questions like that."

Bonny smiles.

"I know. I know. It sounds defensive and cuts off communication. But what do you say when you're caught off guard?" Tony asks.

"I try as best as I can to be open and tell them the truth."

"How do you know how much to share though?"

"I don't always. Sometimes I'm not sure myself how I feel or if I'm going beyond a point where it's helpful to them. It's a challenge to find the proper balance.

Tony looks confused.

Bonny continues, "It's not that there is a right or wrong answer or a certain amount of information that should or should not be shared. It's the realness of the response. If the kids or fellow staff members feel you're hedging, it creates a trust issue."

22

"But what if you don't know?" Tony asks.

"Then that's the real response... For example, sometimes the kids will ask questions about drinking or sex that you haven't thought about or you might have self doubts. If they sense you're trying to cover up, they will continue to do it themselves. But if you are able to question yourself, then they will feel freer to do it themselves."

"But I don't want them to feel the burden of my problems or uncertainty."

"No, you don't. That's the fine line that it takes time to learn how to walk...It's why we talk about it at our team meetings. To give each other a chance to practice. But we also know that if we can't talk about these most difficult issues it will interfere with everything else."

Tony looks puzzled again.

"Imagine trying to make a decision about a home visit for a sexually abused kid or one from an alcoholic system and sitting there feeling as if you can't express yourself because something in your experience makes it hard to talk about. Or you're upset with a fellow team member. Or confused. Then imagine trying to make a team decision with the feeling that the team doesn't care how you feel or is insensitive to your struggle. I've seen team members completely close up because they don't feel they can talk about the difficult issues or that anyone cares."

"Well, what if someone is having problems. Should they be working here?"

"Of course. The chances are good that at any point in time one or another of our colleagues will be struggling with something either related or unrelated to what the clients are going through. A loss. A dependency. A feeling of inadequacy. But don't misread me. Some of these issues can be just as difficult to talk about for people who have not been touched by them. It's all a matter of knowing oneself and how to respond... If someone is struggling beyond our ability to help, of course, then we must see that help is sought elsewhere.

"I see," Tony says.

"Like in most things we do, the challenge is to be empathetic, to understand, to place ourselves in each other's shoes by understanding our own experience."

"How will I ever be able to learn and understand all this?"

"You won't. The key is to always try to understand, to realize the other people see and feel the world from different vantage points, that we as team members have our own struggles and fears. Granted, the children's are often far more severe, but if we can't help each other, how can we help them?" She pauses. "It's okay to be confused."

Independent living conversation cont.

Outside the office Angel (youth who called earlier) joins the independent living group with a slight bruise above the eye. "Oh, good, we're glad you made it," Milly (yw) says.

"Hey, Angel," Nathan (y) slides his chair over so she can sit next to him. The other kids giggle.

"We were just making our rounds," Milly (yw) says.

"You want me to beat the shit out of your boyfriend?" Nathan whispers loud enough for the others to hear.

"Nathan, that won't solve anything."

"I know, but it pisses me off," Nathan (y) moves his chair closer to Angel (y).

"You got to get away from that man," Tanya (y) advises.

"If he really loved you, he wouldn't do that," Nathan (y) says.

"It's not worth it just for the sex," Tanya (y) says. "Look what it got me." She looks down at her baby.

"You're right," Angel (y) says.

"Not all men are assholes," Lamont (y) comments.

"No, of course, they aren't," Milly (yw) responds.

"I'm a nice guy," Nathan (y) jokes and the others laugh.

The group fills Angel (y) in on what they've been talking about and continues the discussion until about 4:30 when Milly (yw) ends the meeting so she can take Angel (y) to the women's shelter.

Supervision cont.

In Bonny's office, Bonny, who is continuing supervision with Tony, says, "We are in many ways like them, the kids, searching, trying to understand ourselves. Our route is different perhaps and we're at different places, but the goal is the same: knowing ourselves..."

Hank, the youth worker, who was talking to the gang leader on the playground, sticks his head in the door, "Guess what?"

"What."

"I got the gang leader to talk to his members about working on the neighborhood clean-up."

"How did you do it?" Milly asks.

"I'm not sure, persistence I think."

"You must have connected in some way. He must have felt a sense of realness, sincerity."

Hank thinks a moment. "When he asked me what was in it for me, I said I wasn't sure. Maybe a chance to prove something, or to do something fulfilling...."

Preparing for Josh's home visit

Across town Jack knocks on Josh's parents' front door. Mrs. Wilson peers through the window, then opens the door and invites him into the living room, which she has straightened somewhat for the visit, but not enough to hide the stuffing coming out of the furniture or the cockroaches in the corner.

"I like the pattern in that dress," Jack says.

"Oh, thank you." Mrs. Wilson seems taken by surprise.

Mr. Wilson walks in, undershirt out, dirty and torn—his eyes glazed.

"I'm glad you're here." Jack turns to Mr. Wilson.

Mr. Wilson frowns.

"Please sit down, Jack." Mrs. Wilson motions towards the couch.

As he sits down, Jack says. "I've talked to the loan company and they said they won't take further action if you at least make some sort of payment each month, even if it's only a few dollars."

Mr. Wilson looks angrily at his wife. To him, accepting help is a weakness. She moves towards Jack, then sits in the chair next to the couch. Mr. Wilson leans against the archway to the dining room, which is cluttered with dirty clothes.

"I've also got some news about a possible job," Jack says.

"What does it pay?"

"Not much, but it's a start..."

Mr. Wilson rolls his eyes.

"Well, we can get back to that. The main reason I'm here is to talk about Josh's visit."

The corners of Mrs. Wilson's mouth raise slightly.

Jack continues, "I want to make sure that he will be safe and that you will take responsibility to see that he doesn't get involved with drugs again."

Mrs. Wilson nods.

"What about you, Mr. Wilson?" Jack asks.

"I won't put up with any of his crap."

"Good, but I have to have your reassurance that you won't do anything physical, that you use some of the discipline methods we talked about."

Mrs. Wilson looks sadly at Mr. Wilson. "Yes, yes," he says.

"It will also help if you have an activity planned... How about going to a football game with him? I have some free tickets." Jack looks at Mr. Wilson.

"We'll see," Mr. Wilson says.

"They're in first place," Jack says.

Supervision cont.

At the headquarters, Tony digests Bonny's last comments. "Thanks for the extra time."

"I enjoyed it, Tony. We'll continue with this next week."

They work on reports and log notes, then go home. Both will return in the morning to get the kids at the group home up for school. Tony will also take Ron, one of the youths at the group home, for one-to-one tonight.

Dinner

Matt returns from the playground to the group home with the three youth with whom he played basketball, Ron, Pat, and Josh. Nicole (yw) is just cleaning off the table with Nick (y) and Jennifer (yw). Monique (y) is in her room, still writing. "Want to see my story?" Nick (y) asks Matt (yw).

"Yes, of course."

As the basketball players sit in the living room, reading magazines, Matt reads Nick's story.

"It's excellent, Nick, especially the way you were able to express how you felt. Maybe you can read it at group tonight."

Nick, who is working with Jennifer (y) and Nicole (yw) to prepare dinner, smiles.

"Read mine?" Jennifer asks.

"Yes, I'd like to, but it will have to be after dinner, okay?"

Jennifer nods.

Nicole (yw) joins the boys in the living room, turns down the music slightly. "It's almost time for dinner," she announces.

"What are we having?" Pat (y) asks.

"Tacos, rice and beans, your favorite," Nicole says.

"Didn't we just have tacos?" Josh (y) asks.

"Two weeks ago... Why, what do you want, burgers again?"

"Nothin' wrong with burgers," Ron (y) says.

"Let's not get into an argument about food... It's almost time anyway. Why don't you start washing up."

Pat and Ron race for the stairs.

"One at a time," Nicole says.

Return

   The squad car pulls up in front of the group home. Franco is being returned from his runaway. Ron, who sees it from the upstairs window, runs to get Nicole and Matt. Franco walks up the sidewalk between the officers, cussing.

Nicole takes a deep breath as she stands with Matt at the door.

"Fuck you!" Franco greets them.

"Watch you language buddy, or we'll take you right back to the detention center," one of the officers says.

Franco is silent.

The officers hand the workers Franco's wallet and some release papers to sign.

Nicole signs the papers.

"Thanks," Matt says.

One officer looks at Franco. "If this continues, you know the judge will lock you up longer than just one night."

"I don't care," Franco says.

"Well, you might want to think about it. Unless you enjoyed these last few hours," the officer responds and then leaves with his partner.

Nicole and Matt escort Franco to his room where he can take off his jacket. Defiantly he follows, "Who the fuck was messing with my room!" he says to the workers who cleaned up the mess he had made before he ran away. They also had the window fixed, which he had broken.

Choosing not to make his seeming lack of appreciation an issue, the workers escort Franco to the bathroom where he can get cleaned up before dinner. But as they turn into the hallway, he bursts down the stairs and out the front door and is gone again. Matt gives chase but is unable to stop Franco.

Before she dials for the police, Nicole says, "It's so frustrating sometimes."

"I know. But we can't make him stay," Matt says.

"What will I tell the police."

"Just tell them we tried to keep him here. They'll understand, I think."

Second home visit (entry)

A few blocks away two workers, Natalie and Ramon from Nexus' In–Home Support program, are getting ready to sit down with the McNights for dinner. Earlier, Natalie helped Mrs. McNight, one daughter, Renee, and a son, Paul, prepare the meal. Ramon helped Mr. McNight, an accountant, get his car fixed. The third child, Jessica, has just arrived from school.

The workers stand on opposite sides of the table. "Shall we sit down?" Natalie (yw) says. This is the first time the family has been together for dinner in a long time.

"God, who wants to eat with them." Jessica (y) folds her arms across her chest.

Mr. McNight, a quiet man, sits down first. The others, except for Jessica, join him.

"Sit down!" Mrs. McNight shouts.

Jessica (y) runs out the door.

"Get back here!" her mother shouts.

Ramon (yw) catches up to her by her father's car. "We'd really like to have you join us for dinner."

"Who wants to eat with them? I hate them."

Ramon sits on the curb. Jessica circles around him for a few minutes, then sits a few feet away.

Shelter

Milly, the independent living worker, is at the shelter with Angel, the girl who was abused by her boyfriend. They have just finished explaining what happened.

"You'll be safe here for a few days. The police have already picked up your boyfriend," Jeff, the shelter worker, says after reading a phone message handed to him by a colleague.

"After that we can arrange for you to stay at the independent living flat until you can get back into your own place," Milly (yw) says.

Angel (y) sobs.

"I know." Milly hugs Angel. "It will work out. I want you to participate in the therapy sessions, okay?" Milly steps back, holding Angel by the arms and looking into her eyes.

Angel nods. As Jeff puts his arm over her shoulder and leads her upstairs to her room, Milly leaves to get a bite to eat before she picks up three youths to take them shopping.

Finishing dinner at the group home

"So where do you suppose Franco is now?," Monique (y) asks.

"With his gang," Ron (y) says.

"Probably cruising," Pat (y) smiles.

"I think he's probably sitting in some alley, cold and hungry," Josh (y) responds.

"I wouldn't want to be out there alone at night," Jennifer (y) says.

"What will happen to him when he comes back? He better be restricted," Monique (y) says. "I was, that time I ran away."

"Let's just hope he comes back okay," Nicole (yw) says.

"Yes, then we'll talk about how we can all help him stay." Matt (yw) switches the subject. "Everyone get enough?"

"I'm stuffed," Monique (y) says.

"You eat like a bird," Ron (y) says.

"Got to keep my figure," she smiles.

"You need some meat on those bones," Ron (y) jokes.

"How's the search for my foster home going?" Nick (y) asks.

"Jack is still trying," Nicole (yw) responds.

"How long does it usually take?"

"It depends how many are available," Matt (yw) says.

"I'm not sure I want to go." Nick (y) slides back in his chair with his arms across his chest.

"I wouldn't," Ron (y) adds.

"Change is frightening," Nicole (yw) says, repeating a comment she made at the group meeting last night.

"Yeah, especially when it's constant," Pat (y) says.

"Yes," Jennifer (y) sighs.

Matt (yw) brings the ice cream to the table.

"What are we doing tonight?" Pat (y) asks.

"Social skills group," Nicole (yw) says.

"Then what?"

"Thought we'd work on our project some more." Matt (yw) bsays.

"Good," Nick (y) says.

Leaving the Wilson's

"I'd invite you for dinner, but I don't have much this evening," Mrs. Wilson says.

"I appreciate the thought," Jack (yw) says, turning on the front stairs. "I'll be here with Josh around noon on Saturday. We can go over what we talked about."

"Yes, thank you," Mrs. Wilson says.

"See you then, Mr. Wilson?"

Mr. Wilson nods.

One-on-one

Tony, who went home for dinner after supervision with Bonny, arrives at the group home to take Ron on a one–on–one. They walk along the bike path next to the river that runs through the center of the city. Often, other children come to the river to hide and play. Not too far away is the park where Ron and his friends used to sell drugs. The police have since cleaned it up. Ahead a work group is cleaning debris. They say hello and walk past.

"So, if you were to follow this path for another two miles you would be at the exit for your job," Tony says, remembering what it was like when he started his first job for pay.

"Cool. Just a straight shot on my bike, man. Sixty miles an hour, two minutes," Ron says.

"Well, probably not that quick, but yes it won't take long and it's pretty hard to get lost. All you have to do is stay on the path, then the restaurant where you'll bus tables is a block away from the exit."

"I know, you showed me in the car last night, man," Ron responds.

"Aren't you a little worried about this job? I know I was when I started my first job."

"Naw, man, it will be cake. Besides, like you said, I'm ready."

"Well ready doesn't mean not being a little anxious."

Ron moves ahead a few paces, turns, "I know man. Sure, I'm a little freaked about it. But I'm excited too. I'll have my own money."

Tony smiles, catches up. "I'm glad you're excited. Mrs. Chin is a nice lady to work for. We've had other kids do well there and I know you will too."

"I'm going to buy me a CD player, man."

"Yeah, but what else?"

"Some of the money is going in savings for design school."

Tony smiles again and they continue walking a little before stopping to sit by the river. Ron looks across the water. "I used to hang in that park."

"I know."

"They cleaned it up."

Tony waits. Ron grabs a stick, holds it out as if there is a fishing line attached. "My dad and I used to catch coho salmon over at the lake. Big suckers." He spreads his hands.

"Yeah, I remember, you told me once."

"That was before they put his ass in prison."

Again, Tony waits. Ron tosses the stick in the water. "I'm glad they cleaned up the park. If my friends were there, I might go back. I don't think so, but I might."

"Yes, it's a strong temptation to go back, but I think you're ready now. You've come a long way since then."

"Yeah, most of them are locked up too now." Ron stands up. Tony joins him back on the path. They walk a while in silence.

"So, tell me again, who gets the tips?" Ron asks.

"The waitresses split them with the bus boys. That's why it's important to do a good job. The sooner you clean their tables, the sooner someone can sit down again and that means more tips. So does having a really clean table. No one likes to pay to go out to eat and find a messy table in front of them when they sit down."

"Tell me some of the names of those orders again?" Ron asks.

Tony runs through the list of some of the dishes at the Chinese Restaurant, most of which are unfamiliar to Ron. Then they turn and begin to walk back.

The sun has set now and there is an orange tint to the sky. They pass without mentioning it again and say hello again to members of the clean-up crew, who have finished and are sitting on the banks

34

waiting for the truck to pick them up with the plastic garbage bags. "Got to go to school so I don't end up like those guys," Ron says.

"Yes, you have tremendous potential in graphic design. Be a shame to see you waste it."

"I won't. Did you like the poster I did for the living room?"

"Yes, it's beautiful. How did you feel about it?"

"I can do better, but it's okay."

"Okay!" Tony jokes, changing the mood.

"Well great by most standards, man. But just a little warm up for me."

They turn off the path towards the group home which is about two blocks east. When they return, Nicole and Matt are sitting on the porch steps with the other kids relaxing after dinner.

Coaxing and Teaching

At the McNight's, Ramon coaxes Jessica back to the table. He speaks in a firm yet caring voice while moving slowly ahead as if gently pulling her along. They join the other family members for dinner. Meanwhile after a quick dinner at a fast food restaurant, Milly (yw) picks up Tanya and Nathan, two of the independent living group members, and takes them to the mall to bargain shop. Nathan immediately finds an expensive pair of tennis shoes.

"What else could you do with the money?" Milly asks.

"Take me out for dinner at a nice restaurant, a movie, and buy me a new dress," Tanya jokes.

"How about pay two weeks' rent." Milly says, placing the shoes back on the shelf.

Homework and dishes

"Let's see if we try it this way," Nicole (yw) leans over Monique's (y) shoulder, helping her with a math problem, while Jennifer (y) works at her desk on the other side of their bedroom. Downstairs in the kitchen, Matt (yw) and Pat (y) dry dishes while Josh (y) puts them away. "Are you excited about the visit?" Pat (y) asks.

"Sure, wouldn't you be?" Josh (y) says.

"I don't know, man. There's a lot of shit that goes on at my house," Pat (y) says.

Matt hands him another dish.

"Yeah, I know what you mean," Josh says.

Jack (yw) walks in from the home visit.

"Josh was just talking about his visit," Matt says.

"Good. I talked to your father. He said he'll go to the football game as long as you listen to what he says."

"Was he sober?" Josh asks.

"Yes."

"He'll probably fuck up, like he always does." Josh places the dish in the cupboard.

"I think he's trying."

"How's my mom?"

"Fine."

"Why don't you two go and talk a little bit. Pat and I will finish up here," Matt says.

"Hey, why does he get out of doing dishes? He's the one with the visit. I'm stuck here this weekend," Pat says.

"C'mon, help your roommate out." Matt nudges Pat.

"You owe me," Pat says.

Jack and Josh step into the office off the dining room.

36

At the mall/family meeting begins

Milly has taken Nathan and Tanya, two of the independent living youths, shopping at the mall. She has just talked Nathan into a less expensive pair of shoes and they are helping Tanya pick out a snow suit for her daughter. After some fussing, Ramon talks Jessica into doing the dishes with him. Natalie goes into the living room with Mr. and Mrs. McNight and the other two children and chats with them while they wait for Ramon and Jessica to start the family meeting.

Restraint

Jack (yw), Nicole (yw), and Matt (yw) are on the floor with Josh (y). During his discussion with Jack about the home visit, he lost it. They aren't sure what triggered his anger other than the fear of being near his father again. "Fuck, I ain't going home. I hate that asshole," he said and threw a book at Jack.

Jack is sitting now with his back against the wall with Josh cradled in front of him. Nicole and Matt are holding his legs. As Josh screams and shouts obscenities, the workers calmly repeat, "We understand how scared you are, but we can't talk about it until you are settled. We are going to stay here and keep you safe until you can do it for yourself..."

"Fuck you!" Josh shouts and twists while Jack, Nicole, and Matt try to hold him securely.

Talking with the community

Hank, meanwhile, is at the grade school for a community meeting where he is reporting the results of his meeting with the gang leader to several neighbors and representatives from community organizations. He has just told them about the gang members' willingness to be involved in the clean-up project.

"I don't want their help," one neighbor says.

"Why not?" Hank asks.

"As far as I'm concerned they don't deserve being acknowledged. If they want to join us as individuals, fine. But not as members of a gang."

"They only join gangs to belong to something. What's wrong if they want to help now instead of causing problems. Maybe it will give them confidence to belong to something worthwhile in the future," another neighbor responds.

"Wanting to belong to something doesn't justify dealing drugs and stealing."

"No. But these aren't bad kids. I've known most of them since they were little... They just haven't gotten any breaks," a mother of one of the gang members says.

As the conversation continues, Hank listens....

Practicing social skills

Josh has stopped fighting and swearing. They are all exhausted. Jack, Nicole, and Matt begin to let go one step at time. "I'm going to let go of one arm... Okay, now the other... Good...Now please go and sit on your chair..." Josh gets up and walks towards the chair. "When you're ready, we can talk," Jack says calmly.

Nicole and Matt take deep breaths and go in the living room with the other youths. After explaining that Josh is okay, they sit on the floor—in much the same fashion as the workers were earlier in the day when they had their team meeting—in the midst of practicing their job interviewing skills.

"Go ahead, you try it now, Pat (y)," Nicole (yw) says.

"I don't want to do that."

"Jennifer and I did it last week," Monique (y) prompts Pat (y).

"Will you help?"

"Yes." Monique stands.

"This seems so fake." Pat, uncomfortable, tries to gather himself.

"I know, but it is important to practice so you can overcome some of the fears you'll have, like the ones you're feeling now," Matt (yw) responds.

"C'mon let's get this over with so we can work on the project," Josh (y) grumbles as he returns.

Pat (y) smiles at Josh (y), "You're next," then straightens himself and extends his hand to Monique. "Hello, my name is Pat."

Monique giggles momentarily before correcting her expression. "Hello, I've been expecting you. Won't you sit down."

Family session cont.

The McNights, appearing equally uncomfortable in their living room, are listening to Ramon and Natalie talk about how important it is not to blame one another, but rather to try to work together by seeing that everyone has a role in the problem as well as the solution. As they speak, their eyes move from one family member to another. Paul and Renee pretend not to pay attention. Jessica has her arms folded across her chest. Mrs. McNight seems frustrated; Mr. McNight remains expressionless.

On the way home

With night falling, Milly, Tanya, and Nathan return from the shopping trip, listening to the radio in Milly's car. She will drop them off, then go home for the evening.

At the school, the neighbors continue their debate about whether or not the gang members should be allowed to help with the clean-up project. The tone seems to have shifted in favor of allowing them to do it.

Angel sits in on a rap session at the shelter. Several other young women about her age sit around her sharing their feelings about being abused.

Art project

After Pat (y) and Josh (y) finish practicing their interviewing skills, Monique (y), Jennifer (y), and Nick (y) read their stories, each one in its own way a rich expression of something—a feeling, an event, a moment—in their lives.

"Can I join your group next week?" Ron (y) asks.

"Of course, we'd be glad to have you," Nicole (yw) says.

"Okay, let's start work on our project." Matt (yw) looks at the clock.

The youths rise to their feet and follow Matt and Nicole to the recreation room. Last night they covered the pool table and painted the wall white. "It's dry," Pat says, after running his finger over the section he had painted.

"Good, now let's look at the drawing and think about the colors we want to use." Nicole unrolls a drawing of the mural they plan to paint and places it on the pool table. They got the idea on a trip to a community center where a Mexican youth worker had helped the neighborhood children paint a large mural on the outside of the building. In theirs, they have decided that each of them will paint something that is symbolic of their ethnic or familial background: a person or holiday or event or food or object. Jennifer came up with the idea to tie it all together with a twisting path. "So we can strut through each other's culture," she demonstrated at the meeting last night.

"Lots of red," Nick says.

"And blue," Jennifer says.

"And yellow," Pat says.

"Yeah, yellow, lots of it," Ron says.

"Okay, but first let's stencil it on the wall. Ron, grab the other end. We'll hold it while Jennifer tapes it," Nicole says.

Jennifer finishes the taping and the youths begin to trace over their lines on the paper, the back of which Nicole has blackened with a pencil. Slowly their work emerges on the wall.

Parenting

Monica, a shelter youth worker, is at 16-year-old Tashita's apartment in the housing center, with Tashita's mother and Tashita's one-year-old son, teaching parenting skills. After a brief stay at the shelter where Tashita and her child were placed after Tashita was abused by her boyfriend, Monica has continued with Tashita at home. The philosophy at the shelter is that it is good to continue these relationships as the women transition back into the community.

Monica kneels on the floor where she is at the child's level. She plays and talks with the child. Tashita's mother watches, then after a while, sensing Monica's sincerity and concern, also gets down on her knees. "Get over here," she says to her daughter, who with a rather disgusted look, walks slowly towards them.

Closing

"Well, I think we have made a good start," Ramon says, closing the family meeting at the McNight's.

"How often do we have to do this," Paul asks.

"As long as you need," Natalie responds.

"Will you always be the two coming?" Jessica asks.

"Yes," Ramon smiles.

"And if any of you need help or just want someone to talk to, please remember you can reach one of us at the number we gave you," Natalie says.

Another closing

"Thank you so much for your help, Hank," one of the neighbors says as they walk across the lighted playground.

"Thank you."

"All they need is a chance to belong to something more worthwhile."

"I agree. I look forward to working with you and the kids this weekend."

The neighbor smiles and gets in her car.

Bedtime

The children at the group home clean up and get ready for bed. As they take showers and prepare their things for the morning, Matt (yw) supervises them and Nicole (yw) prepares the snack. The walls of their rooms on the second floor are covered with posters and pictures and filled with other personal items that express who they are. There are three bedrooms, two children in each one. The girl's bedroom has it's own private bathroom. The boys share one off the hall. As they go through their routines, each one does it in a slightly different way.

Matt helps wherever he can, then announces that the snack is ready: juice and trail mix. They get their snacks from the kitchen, trickle into the living room, and lounge on the furniture, watching television or reading a magazine or book. Matt (yw) sits next to

42

Monique (y); Nicole (yw) next to Pat (y). Monique leans her head on Matt's shoulder and asks him to read. Two others sit on the floor, listening.

When it's time for bed, they grumble a bit, then gradually make their way to their rooms. Pat and Monique get into some horse-play. Matt breaks it up. Ron wants a cough drop. "Yeah, give me one too!" Jennifer says. All in all, considering the fears most of them have about being alone with their thoughts in their rooms, they go to bed pretty well tonight.

Matt and Nicole spend time with each one saying goodnight, giving hugs to some, tucking others in and helping in whatever way they can. In Josh's room, Nicole sits a moment next to his bed. "Do you like the drawing I did for the mural?" Josh asks.

"Yes, very much."

"My grandfather was a Sioux."

"Yes, I know."

"We went there once, to North Dakota. I remember the prairie and the horses."

As he speaks about his trip, then the home visit, Nicole listens, giving him her undivided attention. Before she leaves, she says, "I understand. It's frightening. To risk being rejected again."

Josh rolls towards the wall. She pulls the cover over his shoulder.

Later, Matt and Nicole sit downstairs by the dining room table, writing their logs the way the children wrote their stories earlier, each one a significant event.

About 10:45, John, the overnight person, a college student in his final year of studying to be a youth worker, arrives. They fill him in on the day's events, then leave as he peeks in the kids' doors.

At the local coffee shop, Milly, Hank, and Jack are talking. Matt and Nicole join them. "So, how was your day?" Matt asks. The others smile.

End of day elsewhere

Two youths, Wiley and Jack, are sitting in the basement of an old warehouse. They've lived here for several months and have just run away from two police officers who tried to get them for running drugs.

"Fuck, did you see how I smoked that fat sonofabitch," Wiley says.

"Yeah, you left him man," Jack pauses. "I'm scared, man."

"Of who, the cops?"

"No, not the cops, stupid. Rudolpho."

"Rudolpho?"

"They got our names. Now that we're 16 they can run a criminal record on us as adults. Rudolpho won't let us run his drugs anymore, man. Fuck, he don't need us at all. He can get some younger dudes."

"He'll waste us," Wiley says, reflecting on Jack's comments.

"Fuck yes."

"What should we do now?"

"How the fuck do I know."

"I ain't workin' no minimum wage."

"Me either, not after what we were pullin' down from Rudolpho."

"We're fucked, man."

"Royal. Big time."

"Motha fuck."

"Fuck."

Chapter Three:
Overnight, Morning, and Afternoon

John (YW) sits for a few moments, enjoying the silence of his office at the group home and reading the youth workers' log notes. When he finishes, he walks down the hall looking in on each of the youths. All is quiet.

A few hours later, he hears Pat get up. Still groggy, Pat rests his head on John's shoulder as he walks him to the bathroom. Monique's covers need adjusting and Ron's radio needs to be turned down. John does this and escorts Pat back to his room.

Midnight rap

At the shelter for battered women, Angel has gotten up and is talking with one of the other young women and a youth worker in the living room. They each have a glass of milk.

"I don't know why he hits me. He says he loves me and sometimes he acts as if he does, but how can someone who loves you be so mean?" Angel says.

"Yeah," the other woman says.

"Sometimes people don't love themselves so they take it out on others," the youth worker says.

"But that doesn't make it right, does it?" Angel asks.

"No. Absolutely not. Nor does it mean it's your fault...." the youth worker continues.

McNights follow-through

Earlier, following Ramon's (yw) advice, Mrs. and Mr. McNight insisted in a firm but caring way that Jessica turn out her light and go to sleep. They also tried to assure Jessica by their presence that they would not allow her to sneak out the way she had previously. Now they are in bed, half awake, reflecting on how they did.

Being there in the middle of the night

Back at the group home, Josh has gotten up and is sitting on the couch with John. He had a bad dream but doesn't feel like talking right now.

Morning

When Bonny and Tony (the Nexus group home supervisor and youth worker) arrive at the group home at 6:30 a.m., John is writing logs.

"How did it go?" Bonny asks.

"Pretty good, except for Josh."

"What happened?" Tony asks

"He got up a couple times. He said he had bad dreams." But I think he's really worried about his home visit."

"Did you talk with him?"

"A little bit, but he wouldn't say much. So I just sat with him a while until he went back to sleep." John looks at Bonny.

"You did the right thing," Bonny says. "You acknowledged his feelings and let him know you cared."

John smiles and stands, looking at Tony. "Jennifer and Josh are ready for your run."

"Good." Tony changes in the staff bathroom and gets Josh and Jennifer, who are waiting in their rooms in their running clothes.

They run together down the street. As they catch a second wind, they move easily over the leaves and curbs. Tony jokes and chats with them a bit, but most of the time they just enjoy the motion and clear fall air.

John finishes writing the logs, then leaves for the university where he will attend class before going home to sleep. Bonny begins her rounds, waking each of the youths in a different way. Monique likes a gentle hand on the shoulder, Ron the sound of a radio, Nick the shade raised slightly and so forth. Only Pat, a quick riser, needs instant attention. He wants to know everything that will occur in his day. Bonny obliges, sitting next to him in the hall and running through the school and evening activities while the others slowly open their eyes.

Extra support

Milly has gone to the woman's shelter. Angel is sitting next to her in the living room.

"Thanks for coming, Milly." She leans her head on Milly's shoulder.

"I wanted to be here when you got up. I know how lonely you must be."

Angel nods.

"Maybe if we plan out your day, it will help. You have a lot to look forward to."

Angel nods again, smiling slightly.

A good start.

At the McNight's, Natalie, the youth worker, talks with Mr. and Mrs. McNight, offering tips and assisting them in finding solutions for getting their children up and ready for school. She will observe, teach, and assist in whatever way she can, then talk with the McNights about it at the next family session.

Getting ready for school

While Ron (y) and Nick (y) finish dressing, Bonny (yw) starts breakfast with Pat (y) and Monique (y). Pat puts slices of bread in the toaster; Monique, eggs in the boiling water. Nick shuffles in. "How's it going?" Bonny asks.

"Okay."

"Where's Ron (y)?"

"Finishing a math problem."

"Here, why don't you help Pat while I get the table set," Bonny suggests.

Jennifer (y) and Josh (y) return with Tony (yw) and clean up, then go downstairs with Ron for breakfast. "Everyone finish their homework?" Tony asks as they set the table with plates and food and juice from the refrigerator.

"I did, want to see," Monique says, leaning her body against Tony. He gently places his hands on her shoulders and shifts his position so she is to his side, "Yes, as soon as we finish....What about the rest of you."

They all confirm, except Josh, who remains silent. "Did you finish yours?" Bonny asks.

He nods.

"I'm worried about my geography test, will you help me after breakfast?" Jennifer asks. Josh nods again, this time with a slight smile.

Monique searches for a station on the radio, looking for what they call "morning music."

"Not too loud," Tony says.

"I know."

"I like that outfit, Jennifer," Bonny says.

"Yeah, cool," Ron adds.

Breakfast at the shelter

The shelter workers invite Milly to join them for breakfast. Angel sits next to her. The food is passed in relative silence among the abused women. The workers make a light comment here and there, but mostly attend to serving them and making sure they get enough. The sound of soft music can be heard in the background. Jeff, a shelter youth worker, adjusts the blinds. Sunlight falls on the floor.

Back in the community

Hank, the street worker, is having coffee with Raol, the director of the neighborhood center, a few blocks away from the Nexus headquarters. They are in the new cafeteria, which has been built by the kids and a local builder who volunteered his time. The goal is to use it as a job training site as well as a source of additional income.

"So, I got Nate to agree to have his gang members help with the clean up," Hank says.

"Amazing. What did the neighborhood council say last night?"

"After some discussion, they agreed it was a good idea."

"Sorry I couldn't be there, but I was tied up here."

"It looks great. When's the grand opening," Hank says.

"Tonight."

"I'll be there." Hank pushes his cup aside and leans forward on his elbows. "Will you help with the clean up this weekend?"

"Sure. So will some of the kids and staff," Raol responds enthusiastically.

Getting Angel and the McNights going

After breakfast at the shelter, Angel (y) walks with Milly (yw) to the door. "Okay, you know now what you have to do. I want you to get started right away. Besides if you keep busy you'll feel better," Milly says.

"Can't you go with me?" Angel asks.

Milly frowns.

"I know, I have to take responsibility," Angel responds immediately.

"You got it."

Jeff, the shelter worker, steps in from the kitchen with a few of the other young women, who are going to their rooms to get ready for their day. "Thanks again Milly," he says.

"Yeah, thanks Milly," Angel gives her a hug.

The McNights have all managed to have breakfast together and the kids are ready for school. Natalie is helping with the finishing touches.

Foreshadowing

At the group home, Bonny (yw) and Tony (yw) are sitting in the living room with the kids, finishing their running through the day or foreshadowing.

"So, you're clear now on what will happen today?" Bonny asks.

"When's my doctor appointment again?" Jennifer (y) asks.

Tony looks at the chart on his lap. "2:00 p.m."

"How about football practice?," Pat (y) asks.

"Right after school," Tony responds.

They rise together, the workers positioning themselves for the transition as the youths get the remainder of their clothes and school items.

After they leave, Bonny and Tony sit down in the office together with a cup of coffee. "What time do you have to be at the school?" Bonny asks Tony.

"9:30."

"I thought you did a good job with Monique," Bonny says thoughtfully.

"When?" Tony asks.

"Before breakfast when she leaned against you....The way you positioned yourself without making an issue about it. You were firm, but caring. That's what she needs: men who will not confuse her seductive gestures with her need for nurturing."

"Thanks."

They finish their logs and after picking up a few of the things the kids missed, leave.

Summing up

With Mr. McNight anxiously looking at his watch, Natalie reviews what went on. "Did you notice how I woke them and gave them a few minutes before going back to their rooms. Also how I positioned myself and kept my voice at a steady but firm pace. Not nagging, but reassuring and authoritative....Mr. McNight, did you notice?"

"Oh, oh, yes." He responds, still preoccupied.

"Sit down Gerald, this will only take a minute," Mrs. McNight insists.

Hank and Nate connecting with food

Hank, the youth worker, is with Nate, the gang leader, now on the corner. Nate looks tired. "I talked with Raol at the Center. We're going to get started around 10:00 a.m." Hank says.

"Wooo. That's early, man."

Hank looks at his watch. It's 9:30.

"Yeah, well, I had some business to take care of last night. Otherwise you wouldn't be seeing me this time of day. I'd be with my lady."

"Want to get something to eat?" Hank, who has already eaten but senses Nate could use a good meal, asks.

"Where, man."

"Boxers." Boxers is a home cooking diner a few blocks away.

Nate smiles. "All right, I'll take a chance the brothers won't catch me hanging with you."

Helping at school

Tony has arrived at school where he works with the teachers. Short on help, they are pleased to have an extra hand around, especially someone like Tony, who knows how to work with kids. Today he takes a group of kids from Josh's class, who weren't able to go yesterday, to the museum. They drive in the van, the sound of voices echoing off the sides. "Keep it down, please," he says.

Rapping at the headquarters

Bonny has returned to the headquarters and is returning phone calls to referring agencies. Using the same sensitivity, sense of assurance, and firmness she uses with the kids and staff, she listens attentively and responds directly to each request or concern.

Milly has returned also. She goes through her files and schedule to see who will need assistance. Natalie walks in from the McNight's.

"How'd it go?"

"Oh, it's a bit of a struggle, but I think they're going to come around eventually."

"It's difficult when those patterns of dysfunction become ingrained."

"Tell me about it." Jack, who has just stepped in, says,"Josh's parents have been stuck for at least ten years."

"Yes, so have the McNights," Natalie says.

"That's why it's so important to be patient and to be there until they begin to realize this isn't just going to be another short intervention," Bonny says after hanging up the phone. "They won't begin to take responsibility to change until they feel grounded and they can begin with the trust they feel in you. Intellectually they might understand, but emotionally they have to be able to count on someone so they can begin to count on themselves..." She stops herself, smiles. "Am I lecturing?"

"No, you're right, of course," Milly says and pours Jack a cup of coffee.

Field trip

At the museum, Tony is with about ten kids at the Old Town exhibit. Josh has stayed close to him for most of the morning. "Is this life size?" Josh looks into the window of a model grocery store.

"Yes, why?"

"Everything was smaller back then, wasn't it? Even the doorways."

"Yes. That's a good observation. You might want to include it in your report."

Transition

Natalie goes home to rest. She will be back after school with Ramon to help the McNights and two other families they are working with. Milly goes to the independent living flat to pick up one of the youths for an appointment at the job placement office. Hank is lining up equipment for the clean-up next weekend. On the way to a hardware store where he thinks the owner will donate some shovels and brooms, he runs into a youth who should be in school. He stops and talks to the youth.

Lunch

Jennifer (y), Pat (y), Ron (y), and Nick (y) return to the group home for lunch. Bonny (yw) has prepared it: pasta and soup. Tony (yw) accompanies the youths (Josh and Monique will eat at school with their classmates).

They sit quietly, enjoying the moments away from the hectic schedule of classes. Bonny serves, filling each plate with a medium portion of pasta and a cup of soup. Then she sets the bowl in the middle of the table where they can see there is enough for seconds. Tony slices the Italian bread and sets it on the bread board next to the soup where they can grab it as they please. They share their morning experiences and eat until they have had enough to refuel them for the afternoon. Before they return to school they sit in the living room reading magazines, except for Jennifer who asks Tony to play catch. Next year she's going out for softball. Nick goes over his story again with Bonny, fine tuning it.

"Throw me a grounder," Jennifer says to Tony.

Gaining further community support

Hank has walked the truant youth back to school and is haggling with Mr. Becker, a hard-nosed but good-hearted hardware store owner, about the shovels. "Think of it as a donation to the community. Or, as advertising. Yeah, think of it as an advertising cost," Hank says.

"Every time you need something you come down here!" he complains as he pulls out a couple shovels and hands them to Hank. "What time should I be there to help?"

"10:00 a.m.," Hank smiles.

"Don't know what the neighborhood's coming to anymore," Mr. Becker reflects.

"Times have changed."

"Oh, it was hard in my time too, but we worked."

"These kids would too if they could get decent jobs."

"Most of them never put in a good day's work in their lives."

"I got a couple; want to give them a chance, stocking or helping out around here?"

Mr. Becker, who senses he has put his foot in his mouth, considers Hank's request.

Afternoon

The group home youths, except for Jennifer, who has a doctor's appointment, leave for school. Tony pulls the Van around and meets Jennifer at the front curb. "See you this afternoon," he says to Bonny who waves and goes back to the headquarters where she has an appointment with a local elected official.

Immunizations

At lunch Milly, the independent living worker, taught Tanya how to feed and cloth her baby. Now she's in the rocker she got from the discount store, rocking the baby and showing Tanya how to hold her head up. Tanya watches. Later they will go to the health clinic for immunizations.

Change of shift

Matt, Nicole, and Jack arrive at the group home at 2:00 for a team meeting with Bonny and Tony, who is still at the doctor with Jennifer.

"Well, I think we should begin," Bonny says and looks at Nicole who will be running the meeting today. They rotate leadership at each meeting so that everyone gets a chance to handle the agenda. It is also customary to begin by sharing a personal experience or feeling about the kids or team. They do this and move through some of the procedural items, such as shopping lists, reports, chores, individual treatment plans, and home visits, then focus on Pat's birthday, which is coming up in two weeks.

Birthdays, like all anniversaries, holidays, beginnings, endings, and separations are given special attention at Nexus. They try to make each of these experiences as pleasant and fulfilling as possible.

Tony arrives at about 2:25 and they fill him in, then Jack gives a report on his family visit with Josh's parents. He has some concerns, but still feels it is worth the risk. The others, as they did yesterday, share his concerns and agree again that it is the right choice.

"Before we finish today, I thought we could talk a little about Franco, perhaps explore our role in his running."

"You're not saying it's our fault, are you?" Nicole asks, slightly taken aback.

"No, of course, not. There is no blame. And ultimately it's his choice whether he stays or goes. But often, as you know, in these circumstances there is something in the helping system that more or less feeds the problem. I just thought if we explored what was going on, we might find something we can do differently."

"Well, to be honest, I feel a little relieved when he's gone. And guilty," Nicole says.

Bonny smiles. "Yes, I think we all do."

"Like his parents," Jack says.

They continue their discussion about Franco, then the meeting closes with a review of the evening's activities, including Monique's visit with her foster parents.

As they rise to their feet, the first of the youths arrive. Soon they are all sitting around the living room with a piece of fruit. After a few minutes, Monique runs to the window. "Here they are," she shouts, referring to her foster parents. Nicole greets them at the door while Tony gets Monique's overnight bag.

They exchange a few words, then the foster parents leave with Monique. She stops before she gets in the car and turns back. She does not wave. She simply looks as if storing images to take along.

Chapter Four:
Themes

While reading stories and articles in preparation
for this book, several themes kept reappearing.
In this chapter these themes are described with
excerpts from a few of the writers' works.

Commitment

"You either throw your body and soul into it or forget it.
There can be no compromise"
(Waggoner, 1984,p. 255).

"Over the course of the next five months Darren ran the
gamut of behavior, from running away from our secure
unit, physically assaulting staff with a curtain rod he
ripped off the wall, and punching the walls till blood flowed
from his hands, to being a wonderful, fun loving child who
sought out affection from the staff and contributed actively
in what seemed to be his progress toward becoming emotion-
ally healthy. Despite all my setbacks in my attempts to "cure"
this child, I still vowed to be the one that didn't give up, the
one professional that didn't desert this lonely boy...."
(Rose, 1991, pp. 162– 163).

Being "with" youth

"Youthwork is a way of being in the world with kids...   To
recognize the place of hope in youthwork is to remember that
the present is to be understood in the future more than the
context of the past. Biography and history give way to the
possibility as mediated by choice and decision....

"Youth work should not be lonely; it is always one-on-one,
youth worker-with-youth (group)–"us" or "we"...

"Youthworkers....don't "build trust" mechanically, like
carpenters build houses: they are in the world with youth
and, in so being, disclose trust as fundamental to being
together as persons..."
(Baizerman, 1992, pp. 129–133).

60

"Now...now she lay there sleeping, breathing softly and evenly. I felt a sort of sadness as I watched her sleep. A sense of Helplessness. Not for myself against her, but rather for the fact that I could not do anything to chase away the evils of the world. An enchantress I wasn't. A child care worker I was. I leaned over and pulled her rumpled covers over her arms, softly brushed the tussled hair off her face, and whispered, 'Good night, Anna, see you in the morning"
(Nault, 1987, p. 86).

Attachments

"What I have been most struck with over the past ten years is that these children are unattached and have no significant person in their life. They are children who have been traumatized by many losses which cause them to withdraw from attachments. Their losses, coupled with abusive and 'neglective' interactions with adults, significantly retards their capacity for healthy object relationships....They need someone they can incorporate, who they can learn from and who they can become dependent on so they are able to develop from that person (through ego lending), a concept of self and the knowledge and desire to control themselves..."
(McElroy, 1991, p. 36).

"Care is a very personal experience for both the care giver and the cared for person. Each needs the other. Each, within the process of caring becomes more firmly attached and paradoxically takes on a greater range of freedom from the other"
(Maier, 1987, p. 40).

The long haul

"Despite all the warnings we had received, no one expected her first words that summer to be, 'Get the fuck out of my face you asshole, bitch, slut, whore. I never wanted to come to this dumb–ass stupid camp anyway.' Tasha was coming to what might be the hardest, yet most instrumental, three months in her eight years....

So what were we trying to do with Tasha in a three month period? How were we able to show her that we would be there for her, regardless of how she acted. I believe that consistency and predictability were the keys.

These children, so used to havoc, needed to know that no matter what they did, the staff would not abandon them, nor would we ever lash out and hit them or verbally attack them. For some children, such as Tasha, this took a long time..."

(Tausig 1992, pp.54–57).

Undivided Attention

"....think of an incident where you experienced nurturing care. This would be a moment in your life when you felt a sense of being the one, and only one, who counted at that particular moment...."

(Maier, 1987, pp. 114–116).

Developing beings

"We need to work and relate with children as developing beings....It is important to remind ourselves that the developmental approach does not permit preoccupation with deviant, pathological, or defective behavior....When an

62

individual's affect, behavior, and cognition are evaluated
as distinct processes, care workers can rely on predictable
patterns of developmental progression instead..."
(Maier 1987, pp. 2–4).

Rhythms of daily living

"As everyone, adults and boys alike, takes a seat in the
living room, a new calmer rhythm is set. The more hurried
pace of early morning activity is replaced by a slower, more
relaxed tempo. Voice levels are softened, movements are not
so hurried. It is the adults' responsibility to facilitate this
change in the rhythms of the group..."
(Fahlberg, 1990, p. 172).

"We go crazy all night. Two fights, a few arguments, one
runaway returned by police, a visit from a neighbor who
thinks the kids stole his lawn mower, too many irrelevant
phone calls, not enough food thawed for dinner, an angry
mother, a depressed newcomer and no breaks for us. Ronald
and I struggle through....

Gradually the house starts to fall silent. The radios play
softly. There's the odd giggle and whisper. One by one the
lights go out. It looks as if we made it...."
(Desjardins and Freeman, 1991, pp. 139–144).

Nurturance

At the group home for teen mothers, the staff teaches Milly,
14, how to rock her baby daughter to sleep, then they rock
Milly to sleep....
(Observation at a group home for pregnant teens).

63

Space

"On my first home visit, the boy was so scared that he hid in the crawl space behind his bedroom wall where the roof slanted to the first floor. I tried to coax him out but he wouldn't come. So I went in there and that's where we met"

(story told to the author while jogging with a child and youth care worker, John Sullivan).

"We shape our buildings and they shape us....Territory defines the person....Whatever space supports the work endeavored, the question remains: in which way can spatial factors be altered to further accentuate the process....The wish to be periodically alone and to have space of one's own is not merely a whim with children and adults, it is a human requirement"

(Maier, 1987, pp 59–62).

Special skills

"There was a child at the treatment center who never seemed to be able to find his way into the 'in' group. He was awkward and had very poor social skills.

One day as the child care worker was walking with his group, he noticed this child take a drink of water and blow a long, thin stream from his mouth. Some of the other boys tried to do the same thing but none were as good. That night the worker invented a new game for his group called target spitting"

(Notes From a 1970 Morris Mayer (1957) Workshop).

Closeness

"Leo, the Indian looking boy, is watching TV in the lounge. I try to start a conversation with him. I sit down with him and put my arm around his shoulder. 'Having a lazy day, eh?' I ask. He says, "Yah." Then very naturally and gently, he rests his head on my shoulder. I feel so touched. It's the soft feeling when something inside seems to be melting inside between the kids and me.

I wish I could hug the kids more often, but I must be careful. I must learn small talk also, so I will not scare them. Some kids are afraid they might be melted away. They must be tough and put on hard face. They have learned at a very young age the hardening of the heart..."
        (Phuc Nguyen, 1992, p. 94).

Social environment

"Therefore, at Peper Harrow, a potential new boy, attending his interview, is shown around with immense personal commitment by other boys—so are his parents and social worker. By this action alone, an impression begins to be created that this place belongs to the boys, not just the adults. Under such circumstances the new boy's eyes unaccustomedly widen...."
        (Rose, 1987, p. 30).

Perceptions

Bobby, 12, had blond hair with a young, almost babyish face. Abused, then abandoned early, he was bounced from one foster home to one treatment program to another. When he came to the residential treatment center, he was angry and frightened. He had the language (but not the smarts) of the street.

We began with him as we did with all the boys: by paying attention to his basic safety and nurturing needs. We fed him, taught him how to brush his teeth, and made sure he had clean sheets and warm blankets. We tried to talk with him and hold him safely in the midst of his temper tantrums. We made trips to the art room, played together, and got him ready for school.

It wasn't easy. On a visit to the game room, Bobby pushed a pool stick under the felt cloth and broke the television screen with the eight ball.

Nonetheless, gradually and often grudgingly, he began to change. With our help, he learned how to groom himself and take pride in the way he looked, combing his blond hair away from his eyes several times a day. As he became more adept at ping pong and pool, he accepted the paddles and pool sticks as extensions of his own mastery rather than weapons. We taught him social skills.

During our team meetings we evaluated his progress and talked about our feelings about him. Finally the day came when it was time for him to go on limited off grounds, which meant he could take short trips into the community by himself. As we sat at our team meeting we recalled the difficulty we had had. On my fist trip to the variety store, Bobby tried to steal a bag of candy, then when he got caught, he cussed out the attendant.

Over a nine-month period, however, he had grown and each of us on the team had numerous successful voyages into the community with him. We trusted him and felt he trusted us. So it was a consensus decision that it was time for him to go off on his own.

We told him in the afternoon. The usual procedure was for all the adults to tell a boy together in the privacy of his room and then see if the boy concurred with the decision. Bobby was ecstatic. So were we.

At 4:00 p.m., Bobby ran up to me to see if he could make his first journey alone into the world in several months. "Yes, of course, but what do you plan to do?" I responded.

"Go to the variety store."

"What will you buy?"

"LifeSavers."

I got 50 cents from his bank. "How much change will you be getting?"

He scratched his head. "One, no two, yeah two dimes."

"Good, now I want you back at 4:45 so we can get ready for dinner."

"Sure, sure, I'll be back." He ran down the stairs. I watched from the second–floor window in the game room where the other boys were playing as he literally flew down the street like a bird with new wings.

He returned a few minutes early with a smile that went from ear to ear. I greeted him at the top of the stairs. "Wow, looks like you had a good time."

"Yeah, I did." He held the pack of LifeSavers (minus the two he had on the way home) and the correct change.

"Yes, I can see it was a successful trip. You are even back early."

"Yeah, guess what?"

"What?"

"I got a ride."

My smiled sagged. *"You did, from who, one of the workers?"*

"No, no, you know that bench outside the store."

"Yes, so."

"Well, there was a man sitting there and I told him I was from the Children's Center and I was tired and so he gave me a ride."

"Bobby, how could you do that. Your first trip into the community and now I have to ground you," I said.

"Why?" He seemed surprised.

"How many times have we told you not to take a ride from a stranger."

His face turned red and he began to walk away. Then, after a few paces, he turned back towards me with his fists clenched by his side and shouted. "How the fuck was I supposed to know he was a stranger!"

(Krueger, 1991).

The need to be children

"When I first saw Mary, she looked like a caricature of a hooker...I got to know her as a scared and lonely nine-year-old girl who believed she had to be tough to survive...Mary's treatment plan was simple and uncomplicated. She was treated as a young girl, encouraged to interact with peers on an equal level, encouraged to relax and play, was reassured that she was cared for and safe. As she relaxed and let others in, the veneers and defenses dropped away of their own accord. She emerged as a delightful child who openly sought and responded to affection. As her mood lightened and her need to defend herself declined, a warm smile frequently shone on her face..."

(Al Mayotte, 1989, p. 86).

Culture

"The hospital used a form of milieu therapy whereby the peer group helps to determine the wellness and progress of the patient. Everyone was assigned to a group of boys who would, by consensus, rate one another somewhere along a continuum from severely disturbed to normal. The criteria were based upon behavior in the group...

This all sounds reasonable and fair. Yet the very behavior that the facility considered normal was quite abnormal for an American Indian (Tim). Being self-disclosive, breaking down emotionally in front of others, and relating traumatic experiences are all equated with losing face, shame and humiliation. Tim would never display this behavior before other boys in his tribe, and he certainly could never behave this way in front of Anglos.

In Tim's mind, this was brainwashing. He was being forced to give up his culture and adopt the Anglo culture. He had failed at everything—school, finding a job, even committing suicide. The only shred of self-esteem and pride he had left was his identity as a Native American. How would the other boys in his tribe interpret this behavior? What would his grandfather think of him?

To gain release, he had to display behavior appropriate for mainstream children in therapy. He had to act like a white youth. And, deep down, he knew he was expected to think and feel like a white youth. Indeed this was a form of brainwashing or cultural oppression...

Tim wasn't brainwashed. Eventually he hitchhiked across the country and came to live with us...."

(Weaver, 1990, pp. 65–67).

With families

> "Barbara was a 15-year-old Native Canadian girl....Her relationship with her family was characterized by alienation and isolation. As part of the regular unit program, family members spent time visiting with their children and were involved in ways in which they had something to contribute to the group. Barbara's mother showed a desire to be involved. She played guitar very well and liked to sing many of the old, and some of the more contemporary, western tunes. As her way of participating in the program, she came regularly to the unit, and played her guitar and sang for those youngsters who were interested...
>
> Barbara and her mother did not live happily ever after but through this experience Barbara found a way to appreciate and value her mother as a person. They found a way to share an enjoyable experience and now one sometimes finds them together singing and playing new songs or learning old ones from each other"
>
> (Garfat, 1990, p 125–126).

Rhythmicity

> "Have you noticed that when people jog, dance or throw a frisbee in rhythm with each other, they seem to experience momentary bonding and a sense of unity? At these and other moments of joint rhythmic engagement, they discover an attraction for each other regardless whether there has been a previous sense of caring. In fact, it is almost impossible to dislike a person while being rhythmically in "sync." Rhythmic interactions forge people together. Rhythmicity provides a glue for establishing human connections...."
>
> (Maier, 1992, p. 7).

70

Milieu

*"Our major concern is the 23 hours outside the psycho-
therapy session, because that is where the milieu is"*
(Trieschman, et al, 1969, p. 1).

*"...these children live in unique worlds of their own experi-
ence. They are caught up in their own confusion, their own
pain, and their own rage. From this perspective, the task is
coming to know, understand and respect the world of each
child, skillfully and diligently helping the child to move
through the torment and learn ways of expressing herself,
himself, in the world....*
(Fewster,1993, p. vii).

*"It was bedtime and as I said goodbye each boy wished me
the best, wanted me to write and send photos. Only Erik
remained quiet, with that well known angry expression on
his face. At last I came to his bed. I told him I would miss
him and that I would write. He remained motionless with
his arms crossed tightly against his chest. As I looked down
at him to say my last goodbye, he suddenly reached up and
grabbed on to me with his arms around my neck and said,
"Norman, I don't want you to leave," and he began to cry
very sadly. At this point the tears that had been welling up
in my eyes began to roll slowly down my cheeks.*

*This little boy, who according to the experts, was 'not
capable of expressing appropriate feelings and developing a
positive relationship' was expressing sadness and caring"*
(Powell, 1990, p 20).

Crises

> *"Crises are opportune times for adults to model and teach social and emotional competence....For children under stress we must interpret adult intervention as an act of support and protection rather than hostility....We must acknowledge and accept the feelings of children without necessarily accepting the way in which they choose to express them"*
> (Powell, 1990, p. 26).

Peer support

> *"Helping a young person with problems requires that he develop feelings of self-worth, of significance, of importance to others, of dignity, of desire to do good and be good. It includes an examination of one's own behavior in relation to the reactions of others in an atmosphere where the group intent is to help and not to hurt. It includes intensive exposure to a subculture permeated with the positive values of respecting and helping others as well as self respect"*
> (Vorrath and Brendtro, 1974, p. 5).

The power of relationships

> *"Vera rested in the infirmary. Her normal robust body was weakened by the flu. Her bleary eyes caught the movement at the edge of her vision as she lethargically turned to see Kate entering the room. In her twenties, Kate was lean and earnest. She asked Vera how she was feeling, but when she saw the abruptness bordering on contempt with which Vera responded to her, she wondered how she could get Vera to accept her again. She had come to appreciate, to know, and to love this child, whose intelligence, maturity, and linguistic ability enabled her to dominate the group of girls for*

whom Kate was responsible (at the school for the deaf)....

At the Thanksgiving recess her parents, however, had met Kate for the first time, and by the time Vera was returned they had made it clear to the child (Vera) and to Kate that they disapproved of Kate, not wanting their child's worker to be a hearing person. They were as adamant in their position as parents active in civil rights or ethnic identity issues might have been. Vera's old suspicion and ridicule of Kate was renewed and intensified with hostility and defiance...

In talking with Pam (her supervisor) later that evening, Kate was able to express her sense of loss. She discovered how powerful this was, how it dominated her behavior. It felt to Kate as if she herself had done something wrong and must find a way to compensate for her wrongdoing. Pam helped her to see that she had done nothing wrong, and to explore the profound feeling that created a distance between her and the child. Perhaps much of the power of those feelings was not hers but belonged to Vera....

When Kate visited Vera the next day, she had the strength to insist that Vera attend to her, that Vera look at her and "listen." Kate was able to present her sympathetic view of Vera's problem. She saw Vera as having felt she had to choose between Kate and her mother, and that Vera had made the only choice possible. Kate said that she had learned how important it was for Vera, and that it could be understood and she did not, would not, want Vera to risk losing her mother's love. She hoped that Vera could find a way for them to be friends again, but could understand and accept the situation if that was not possible. She told Vera that perhaps her own painful feelings taught her what Vera was afraid of. Vera Wept. They both wept. The conflict cycle had been broken in a climate of warmth and truth"

(Cohen, 1990, pp. 104–109).

Creative expression

"Daniel slowly sauntered to the middle of the stage. He had on black running tights. Painted across his chest and arms were wisps of black and yellow. His face had similar markings fanning across his eyes, nose, and mouth. It reminded me of a Franz Klien expressionist painting.

He jumped into the music and showed us some new stuff. He was neither Mephisto nor Marcel Marceau. He was an ice skater, feet flying effortlessly across the wooden floor. A Spanish dancer, feet stomping, head thrown back, chest thrust out, and arm in half circle overhead...

Soon it became obvious he was painting a canvas to Stillwater's aching harmonies....For me the messages were obvious: he was letting go of Carla, cradling the child he never got to see, and exorcising the last remnants of a violent father. For those who didn't know him, his sadness had to be felt if not understood. Every moment seemed to be spontaneously choreographed to convey his despair, to soothe his pain, to free his anger, to fill an emptiness. It was a painfully beautiful thing to watch. Sue had been right about the healing qualities of dance"

(Krueger, 1987, pp. 134–135).

"I assured Andy that I believed him and he went on with his story. When he vomited, they banged his head against the wall. He was sent to the bathroom to clean up. When his mother came home she beat him for getting feces on her towels. Andy drew separate pictures of his stepfather and his friend and I allowed him to smear brown clay on their faces, so, as Andy put it, "They can know what it feels like to have shit on their faces!" He went back to his footprint pictures

and drew a jail with thick bars on the windows, and put two men in prison for life. In the next picture Andy's mother was beating him across the back with a studded belt. He swiftly changed the belt into a blanket and said, "It's hard to hurt a kid with a soft blanket."

He sat beside me in my bean bag chair in my office, his head resting on my shoulder, wondering why his mother hit him so much...."

(Meyer, 1991, p. 88).

Shared journeys

"Child and youth care workers appear as fellow travelers along the pathway for an increasing number of children in our society. For brief periods of time they share part of their respective journeys, eventually choosing to part company to pursue their own purposes and destinies. The encounters are as varied as the wayfarers themselves, but they all offer their own unique opportunities for each individual to learn from the shared experiences of the others.

The caring adult, as the more seasoned adventurer, has much to offer in the sharing of past struggles and discoveries. Along with these experiences there are also fears, hopes, and aspirations about what lies ahead. Those who journey with calm confidence and courage know that the possibilities and potentials are endless and that each person must learn to steer his own course and make his or her own choices along the way...."

(Fewster, 1991, p. 85).

"Charlotte was inviting me to consider the idea that self-examination and discovery is a process of observing the "self" in action. The idea is that when we are experiencing another person, particularly at a feeling or emotional level, we are actually experiencing ourselves..."

(Selected quotes from Fewster, 1990).

"When you work with troubled children, it is not their reality that you wander: it is your own. Those footprints you see around you are on the border of your own reality, not theirs. Tread gently and with caution but do not be led by your fear. For in the territory of the children's reality, just where it borders with your own, lies the opportunity for change: for them and for you."

(Garfat, 1991, p. 159).

"The 'truth' to be discovered is the revelation of what is, rather than the attainment of should be or the illusion of what might be. In peeling back the layers of their own experience, child and youth care workers can make a unique contribution to our understanding of how it really is to work with kids. They can tell the untold stories of childhood and adolescence, albeit from the 'truth' of their own perspective. Surely the time has come for us to re-examine our discipline that moves from the inside out...look in the mirror, look beyond and tell it as it is."

(Fewster, 1991, p. 62).

Exploration into the complexity of the mind.

> *"The challenge of this field is the ongoing exploration into the complexity of the human mind. Initially, you learn about your feelings of vulnerability and helplessness when you reach out to others, only to experience rejection and abuse from them. Next, you learn about the personal historical luggage which you carry into every new relationship. Then you discover the dynamics of the conflict cycle, aggression and counter aggression, passive aggressiveness and dependency. What's exhilarating to acknowledge is that there is no end to self-learning. In fact, once you understand some complex relationship or achieve some insight into your dynamics, like a co-dependency, the result is a new and deeper list of questions and concerns.…"*

(Long, 1991, p 49).

Conflict

> *"I rushed to the staff bathroom and quickly, but gently, splashed cold water on my throbbing face. I looked into the mirror. For a splash of a second I wanted to ask myself what I was doing here—in this position, in this job. But I didn't have time to be reflective. My red, swollen, teary–eyed face stared back at me and reminded me that I had to get back out there with the kids. Hopefully my nose wasn't broken.…*

> *"Wasn't I supposed to be the strong-you-can-always-count-on-me adult? The one who could control these girls, using physical restraint if necessary when they couldn't control themselves. Wasn't I supposed to hold that girl without hurting her until the rage subsides.… So what happened? What about my own rage, my own hurt. I looked in the*

77

mirror. There it was, already outlining itself on my face...

"My own confusion about what I was feeling made me leery of facing Anna. Anna was the most disturbed child we had in treatment.... All I knew was that there was something eerily contagious about Anna's sick rage....I'm afraid, unintentionally"

(Nault, 1987, p. 81).

Learning from Youth

Some years ago, when I began working as an expressive arts therapist in a residential treatment center for latency age children, I thought of my childhood as safe and protected....However, as the children came to therapy weighed down by conflicts, my carefree early days faded and I was confronted on a new level with unresolved conflicts from my own childhood which I felt had been left behind or forgotten.

The children left me no choice. I could stay on the surface or, through art work and sand play, enter inner lands where I might view the world from behind their eyes, and feel the pain and sadness they were experiencing...

At the onset of my work with victimized children, I was willing to leave my early conflicts undisturbed. But when the children slowly and sometimes shyly gave me permission to step into their inner worlds, without knowing it, they gave me a very special gift. A chance to recapture my own childhood from the mists of the past"

(Meyer, 1991, p. 83).

Chapter Five:

Summary and
Challenge for the Future

At-risk youth need people they can count on. People who are there in the moment and over the long run. People who are sincere, accepting, genuine, dedicated, and self-aware.

They also need people who are sensitive and have the capacity to meet their developmental needs. Growth and trust cannot be coerced, hastened, or forced. They are byproducts of relating to and learning with youth at a pace that is consistent with their abilities and readiness to change.

It takes energy, creativity, knowledge of human development, skill, self-awareness, and teamwork to weave care, learning, and counseling into daily interactions. It also takes practice, patience, persistence, and compassion.

Many metaphors apply. For instance, child and youth care is a modern dance in which worker(s) and youth(s) move in and out of sync. It is also a conversation in which the eye contacts, tones of voice, body position and moments of silence are as important as the proper words. Or a basketball game, the tempo and action changing.

There are no quick fixes. It takes as long as it takes for each youth. One of the greatest injustices today is the claim by some that they can change most troubled youth quickly by altering or controlling a few behaviors without regard for the time it takes for attachments and relationships to form and for change to occur from within.

The work is interactive. Goals and outcomes are important, but the bulk of growth takes place in the process of getting there.

One can never experience exactly what another experiences, but child and youth care is very much a process of trying to understand how children feel (e.g., to be frightened and sad) and thinking about how hard it is to respond when one feels this way (e.g., listen to instruction, piece thoughts together, and gather the energy and feeling of self-worth needed to interact with others), then reconsidering one's expectations.

There is tremendous power and enjoyment in the quiet moments sitting together reading on a couch, the combed hair, the expressed feeling, the silence, and the shared rhythm and play. Much can also be learned from the periods of struggle: the intensity, sweat, work, and drudgery. Moments of joy, harmony, and peace don't exist without these other moments.

The way workers interact with one another is interconnected with their interactions with the youths. In other words, when they praise, encourage, confront, and accept one another, they are more likely to be able to do it well with youths and their families.

Group work is to a large degree selecting activities for a group that address as best as possible the individual needs of each youth, then being sensitive to those needs while conducting the activity and making sure each youth has a chance to experience some success. When group work goes well, it is dance at its finest. Worker in the middle of the group, worker at the edge. Lights up; lights down. Tones of voice softening, then rising. Eyes moving from one partner to the next. Dancing close, then apart. Some of this can't be taught. It's instinct, knowing where to be, where to look, where to walk, when to speak. Some do it naturally, others have to practice and experience it over and over to get it right.

Youths need many ways to express themselves, including music, art, drama, and play. They also need touch—a hand on the shoulder, a hug, a playful nudge that is given with sensitivity to their readiness for physical closeness.

Fear is part of the work for worker and youth. The challenge is to understand, manage, and overcome as much as possible. It takes courage.

Separation and loss are major sources of troubled youths' depression, fear, anger, and sadness. They have been abandoned more than other children. Successful beginnings, endings, and transitions—a smooth walk from one room to another, pleasant greetings, reassuring partings, and discussions of things to come—help youths learn to let go and reconnect with others.

Although little is known about what actually forms the glue in human connections, rhythm, presence, meaning, and atmosphere appear to be key elements. One of the more intriguing questions in child and youth care is how are these elements interconnected?

Realness it seems comes mostly from the quest to understand one's self. Youths seem to know instinctively when workers are sincere and truly present.

Some of it, of course, will also always be a mystery. Baizerman (1992, p. 132) writes:

> *"To recognize the place of hope in life and youth work is to remember that the present is to be understood in the context of the future more than the past. Biography and history give way to possibility as mediated by choice and decision. Let some of this be mystery, not subject to reductionist analysis and control. Some aspects of youth work must remain ineffable, in that sense mysterious—not to be used as an excuse for not knowing what we are doing and why, not as a way to avoid precision and rigor in our thought and honor in our actions, but simply as recognition that youthwork is a form of life, charmed and touched by mystery and wonder. And that is part of the reason why we are needed, and why we are helpful."*

Portage: A Challenge for the Future

They left the group home in midafternoon, but the ride to the campsite took longer than they thought and they had to set up in the dark, sorting tent poles and stakes by feel. There were five boys along with the leader, Kent, a young man in his mid-twenties.

As they settled into their sleeping bags, the sounds of the night scared a few of the boys, who had not been camping before. Kent talked with them until eventually they all fell asleep.

In the morning, Kent got up early to prepare breakfast. The boys woke to the smell of bacon. A couple boys fought over a pair of socks and one got up in a usual bad mood, but as they ate and huddled together by the fire, they gradually eased into the day together.

Afterwards, they cleaned up and reviewed the map they had made for their trip. They would follow a chain of lakes as far as they could, then portage to another lake that ran into a river and flowed south towards a town where arrangements could be made to pick them up and haul them back.

By midmorning everything was packed. They kicked dirt on the coals in the fireplace and pushed away from shore with the wind at their backs. Kent steered one canoe; Daniel, a rugged sixteen-year-old, the other. Soon they had passed from one lake to a second in the chain of six.

Some of the boys got tired and began to complain. Kent tried to slow the pace and keep their minds off their aching muscles by leading a few songs. It worked for a while.

In the third lake they slid their canoes on a sandy beach for lunch. Hungry, they devoured the sandwiches, then afterwards, some of the boys napped while the others waded in the cool early summer water.

When they started out again in the canoes, their arms and shoulders ached. It was a warm ache though and they sang again as they moved through another lake in midafternoon. But eventually, some of the boys began to complain and argue again. Kent knew it was not good to push them. Canoeing was hard work, especially for children who had short attention spans and low frustration levels.

He stopped on an island in the fifth of the six lakes. He let them relax and roam about before setting up camp and preparing dinner. Tired, the boys all went to bed after dinner and a few unusually quiet moments by the fire, which seemed to hypnotize them.

Kent stayed up a while, thinking it was better in some ways in the woods than at the group home. Nature somehow brought them closer together. Out here they had no choice but to trust one another and work together.

It rained most of the night. In the morning the wood was too damp for a fire so they ate a dry breakfast. After crossing the remainder of the lake, they entered a much larger lake where a strong wind began to blow in their faces. They were exhausted by the time they began the portage. The path had grown over and they began to trip and stumble.

"Fuck!" Daniel tossed the canoe to the side and walked into the woods.

"Get back here!" Kent shouted.

"Fuck you! You don't know where you're going."

Kent walked towards Daniel. "I said get back!"

Daniel threw a punch. Kent ducked, then grabbed Daniel and collapsed with him to the forest floor, cradling his body safely the way he had been taught. The other boys watched from a distance. The struggle continued for several minutes until the tension slowly subsided.

As he said, "Okay, I'm going to let go," Kent's voice shook. He thought about this as he regained his composure. His anger and fear had stirred something deeper within him. Daniel seemed to sense this as he stopped fighting.

They rose slowly and joined the other boys, who seemed relieved. When they started out again, they moved ahead to the next lake.

In this story, as in all the previous examples, the emphasis is on self (worker and youth) in action. In other words, focus is on worker with youth in the world (daily living environment). Worker and youth being "real." Worker and youth acting with meaning. Worker and youth becoming aware. Worker and youth in and out of sync with each others' rhythms for trusting and growing. Worker and youth focused on the moment. Worker and youth in space, time, and surroundings. And worker, through being and acting in harmony with self while weaving care and learning into daily interactions, teaching and empowering youth.

This is where the focus of youth work should be today.

> *"I am not looking back, but I am remembering, remembering so many,"*
> (Simons, 1992, p 79).

References and Suggested Readings

Austin, D., & Halpin, B. (1989). The caring response. *Journal of Child and Youth Care.* 4(3), 1–7.

Baizerman, M. (1992). Book review of Buckets: Sketches from the youthworker's log book by Mark Krueger (1990). *Child and Youth Care Forum*, 21(2), 129–133.

Beker, J., & Eisikovits, Z. (Eds.) (1992). *Knowledge utilization in residential child and youth care practice.* Washington DC: Child Welfare League of America.

Beker, J., Gittelson, P., Husted, S., Kaminstein, P., & Finkler–Adler, L. (1972). *Critical incidents in child care: A case study book.* New York: Behavioral Publications.

Brendtro, L., & Ness, A. (1983). *Re–Educating troubled youth.* New York: Aldine.

Brendtro, L., Brokenleg, M., & Van Bockern, S. (1990). *Reclaiming youth at risk.* Bloomington, IN: National Educational Services.

Bronfenbrenner, U. (1979). *The ecology of human development.* Cambridge, MA: Harvard University Press.

Bruner, J. (1990). *Acts of Meaning.* Cambridge, MA: Harvard University Press.

Burmeister, E. (1961). *The professional houseparent.* New York: Columbia University Press.

Cohen, G. (1990). Vera. In M. Krueger & N. Powell (Eds.) *Choices in caring: Contemporary approaches to child and youth care work.* Washington, DC: Child Welfare League of America.

Condit, D. (1989). *The hummingbird brigade.* Taos, NM: Amador Press.

DESJARDINS, S., & FREEMAN, A. (1991). OUT OF SYNCH. *JOURNAL OF CHILD AND YOUTH CARE.* 6(4), 139–144.

FAHLBERG, V. (1990). *RESIDENTIAL TREATMENT: A TAPESTRY OF MANY THERAPIES.* INDIANAPOLIS: PERSPECTIVES PRESS.

FAYE, M. (1989). *SPEAK OUT.* TORONTO: PAPE ADOLESCENT RESOURCE CENTER.

FELICETTI, T. (1987). CONVINCING CARE STAFF TO USE THEIR SELVES. *RESIDENTIAL TREATMENT FOR CHILDREN AND YOUTH.* 5(2), 59–60.

FEWSTER, G. (1990). *BEING IN CHILD CARE: A JOURNEY INTO SELF.* NEW YORK: HAWORTH.

FEWSTER, G. (1993). THE OTHER TWENTY THREE YEARS. *JOURNAL OF CHILD AND YOUTH CARE.* 7(3), VII.

FEWSTER, G. (1991A). THE PARADOXICAL JOURNEY: SOME THOUGHTS ON RELATING TO CHILDREN. *JOURNAL OF CHILD AND YOUTH CARE.* 6(4), V–IX.

FEWSTER, G. (1991B). THE THIRD PERSON SINGULAR: WRITING ABOUT THE CHILD CARE RELATIONSHIP. *JOURNAL OF CHILD AND YOUTH CARE WORK.* 7, 55–62.

GARFAT, T. (1990). A WOMAN WITH HER GUITAR. IN M. KRUEGER & N. POWELL (EDS.). *CHOICES IN CARING: CONTEMPORARY APPROACHES TO CHILD AND YOUTH CARE WORK.* WASHINGTON, DC: CHILD WELFARE LEAGUE OF AMERICA.

GARFAT, T. (1991). FOOTPRINTS ON THE BORDERS OF REALITY. *JOURNAL OF CHILD AND YOUTH CARE.* 6(4), 157–160.

KRUEGER, M. (1987). *FLOATING.* WASHINGTON, DC: CHILD WELFARE LEAGUE OF AMERICA.

KRUEGER, M. (1990). *IN MOTION.* WASHINGTON, DC: CHILD WELFARE LEAGUE OF AMERICA.

KRUEGER, M. (1991). *BUCKETS: SKETCHES FROM A YOUTHWORKER'S LOG BOOK.* WASHINGTON, DC: CHILD WELFARE LEAGUE OF AMERICA.

KRUEGER, M. (1991). COMING FROM YOUR CENTER, BEING THERE, TEAMING UP, INTERACTING TOGETHER, MEETING THEM WHERE THEY'RE AT, COUNSELING ON THE GO, CREATING CIRCLES OF CARE, DISCOVERING AND USING SELF, AND CARING FOR ONE ANOTHER: CENTRAL THEMES IN CHILD AND YOUTH CARE. *JOURNAL OF CHILD AND YOUTH CARE,* 5(1), 77–87.

LONG, N. (1991). AN INTERVIEW. *JOURNAL OF CHILD AND YOUTH CARE WORK.* 7, 49.

MAIER, H. (1987). *DEVELOPMENTAL GROUP CARE OF CHILDREN AND YOUTH.* NEW YORK: HAWORTH.

MAIER, H. (1991). AN INTERVIEW. *JOURNAL OF CHILD AND YOUTH CARE WORK.* 7, 53.

MAIER, H. (1992). RHYTHMICITY–A POWERFUL FORCE FOR EXPERIENCING UNITY AND PERSONAL CONNECTIONS. *JOURNAL OF CHILD AND YOUTH CARE WORK.* 8, 7–13.

MAYER, M. (1958). *A GUIDE FOR CHILD CARE WORKERS.* NEW YORK: CHILD WELFARE LEAGUE OF AMERICA.

MAYOTTE, AL. (1989). MARY. *JOURNAL OF CHILD AND YOUTH CARE WORK.* 5, 75–79.

MCELROY, J. (1988). THE PRIMARY CARETAKER MODEL: A DEVELOPMENTAL MODEL FOR MILIEU OF CHILDREN AND ADOLESCENTS. IN R. SMALL & F. ALWON (EDS.). *CHALLENGING THE LIMITS OF CARE.* BOSTON: THE TRIESCHMAN CENTER.

MCELROY, J. (1991). LETTER TO RICK SMALL. *JOURNAL OF CHILD AND YOUTH CARE WORK.* 7, 36.

MEYER, M. J. (1991). TROUBLED CHILDREN TEACH US A LOT ABOUT OURSELVES. *JOURNAL OF CHILD AND YOUTH CARE WORK.* 7, 81–94.

NAULT, S. (1987). MAYBE I'M NOT CUT OUT TO BE A CHILD CARE WORKER AFTER ALL. *JOURNAL OF CHILD AND YOUTH CARE WORK.* 3, 81–86.

NGUYEN, P. (1992). JOURNAL AT THE SHELTER. *CHILD AND YOUTH CARE FORUM,* 21(2), 91–104.

ORTIZ, S. (1992). *WOVEN STONE.* TUCSON: UNIVERSITY OF ARIZONA PRESS.

POWELL, N. (1990). THE CONFLICT CYCLE: A USEFUL MODEL FOR CHILD AND YOUTH CARE WORKERS. IN M. KRUEGER & N. POWELL (EDS.). *CHOICES IN CARING: CONTEMPORARY APPROACHES TO CHILD AND YOUTH CARE WORK.* WASHINGTON, DC: CHILD WELFARE LEAGUE OF AMERICA.

RANFT, V. (1989). ON EARTH ONE SEES ALL SORTS OF THINGS. *JOURNAL OF CHILD AND YOUTH CARE WORK.* 5, 5.

REDL, F. & WINEMAN, D. (1951). *CHILDREN WHO HATE.* GLENCOE, IL: FREE PRESS.

REDL, F. & WINEMAN, D. (1957). *CONTROLS FROM WITHIN: TECHNIQUES FOR TREATMENT OF THE AGGRESSIVE CHILD.* NEW YORK: FREE PRESS.

REDL, F. (1959). STRATEGY AND TECHNIQUE OF THE LIFE SPACE INTERVIEW. *AMERICAN JOURNAL OF ORTHOPSYCHIATRY,* 29, 1–18.

REDL, F. (1966). *WHEN WE DEAL WITH CHILDREN: SELECTED READINGS.* NEW YORK: FREE PRESS.

ROSE, L. (1991). ON BEING A CHILD CARE WORKER. *JOURNAL OF CHILD AND YOUTH CARE.* 6(4),161–167.

ROSE, M. (1987). THE CONTEXT FOR PSYCHOLOGICAL CHANGE IN A THERAPEUTIC COMMUNITY FOR ADOLESCENTS. *RESIDENTIAL TREATMENT FOR CHILDREN AND YOUTH.* 5(1), 29–43.

SIMONS, P. (1992). CRISIS CENTER. *CHILD AND YOUTH CARE FORUM.* 21(2), 77–80.

TAYLOR, H. (1991). PIECES OF LORETTA'S MIND. *JOURNAL OF CHILD AND YOUTH CARE WORK.* 7, 98–99.

TAUSIG, H. (1992). TASHA. *JOURNAL OF CHILD AND YOUTH CARE WORK.* 8, 54–58.

TRIESCHMAN, A. (1983) ANGER WITHIN: VIDEO TAPE INTERVIEW. WASHINGTON DC: NAK PRODUCTIONS.

TRIESCHMAN, A., WHITTAKER, J., AND BRENDTRO, L. (1969). *THE OTHER TWENTY–THREE HOURS.* NEW YORK: ALDINE.

VANDERVEN, K. (1990). ORIGINS OF MY CAREER IN CHILD AND YOUTH CARE WORK: THE 4 C'S PATHWAY. *JOURNAL OF CHILD AND YOUTH CARE WORK.* 6, 68–79.

VORATH, H., & BRENDTRO, L. (1974). *POSITIVE PEER CULTURE.* NEW YORK: ALDINE.

WAGGONER, C. (1984). FIRST IMPRESSIONS. *CHILD AND YOUTH CARE FORUM.* 12(4), 255.

WEAVER, G. (1990). THE CRISIS OF CROSS–CULTURAL CHILD CARE. IN M KRUEGER & N. POWELL (EDS.). *CHOICES IN CARING: CONTEMPORARY APPROACHES TO CHILD AND YOUTH CARE WORK.* WASHINGTON, DC: CHILD WELFARE LEAGUE OF AMERICA.

Videos

For further insight into understanding child and youth care work with at-risk and troubled children, readers might also find the following videos helpful:

Streetwise
A movie of interviews with and stories about street children in Seattle.

My Life as a Dog
A movie about a troubled child who fears the loss of his mother.

Menace II Society
& Boys of the Hood
Two movies about growing up in poverty and the influence of gangs.

The Breakfast Club
A movie about a group of adolescents who share their feelings and insights while serving a high school detention .

Salaam Bombay
Pixote
Very painful, yet insightful movies about street children in India and Brazil, respectively.

What's Eating Gilbert Grape
A warm movie about family and sibling care under difficult circumstances.

A River Runs Through It
A movie about a family who love one another but cannot keep one of its members from going astray. The book by Norman McClean, of course, is even better than the movie.

Walking Through The Storm
A video providing insights and techniques for working with aggressive youth.

Speak Out
A video about young adults who are working to be independent through writing and telling their stories.

About the Author

Mark Krueger, PhD, is a professor and director of the Child and Youth Care Learning Center, University of Wisconsin-Milwaukee. Prior to coming to the University, he was a child and youth care worker for eleven years. Among the other child and youth work books he has written are four textbooks, *Intervention Techniques for Child and Youth Care Workers*, *Job Satisfaction for Child and Youth Care Workers*, *Careless to Caring for Troubled Youth*, *Choices in Caring*; two novels, *Floating* and *In Motion*; and a book of short stories, *Buckets*. He has also contributed several articles to child and youth care journals, spoken and conducted workshops at child and youth care conferences throughout the US and Canada, and is past president of the National Organization of Child Care Worker Associations.